"Jim Robinson is one of the rising stars in speechwriting today — an accomplished wordsmith in a day when words mean everything. His experience is indispensable to beginners and veterans alike. Whoever are the great communicators of tomorrow will have read carefully the advice of Mr. Robinson."

Kenneth L. Khachigian
Former Speechwriter to Ronald
Reagan and Richard Nixon

"Jim Robinson has a unique ability to communicate succinctly, directly, to the point, and powerfully. He commands and holds the interest of his readers and listeners."

Edwin D. Dodd
Chairman Emeritus and Director,
Owens Illinois

"Jim Robinson is that rare individual who has substantive knowledge of communications, as well as the unique ability to present his ideas logically, clearly, and persuasively."

Richard W. Rahn
Vice-President and Chief Economist,
U.S. Chamber of Commerce

"I've been a businessman and a Congressman, and in both fields communicating is the key — and Jim Robinson is the best! Heed his words. He'll make you a winner, too!"

Rep. Jerry Solomon (R-NY)

Winning Them Over

How to Order:

Quantity discounts are available from Prima Publishing & Communications, Post Office Box 1260JR, Rocklin, CA 95677; Telephone: (916) 624-5718. On your letterhead, include information concerning the intended use of the books and the number of books you wish to purchase.

WINNING THEM OVER

Get Your Message Across by:

- **Dealing Successfully with the Media**
- **Giving Powerful Speeches**

James W. Robinson

 Prima Publishing and Communications
Post Office Box 1260JR
Rocklin, California 95677
Telephone: (916) 624-5718

Editor: Suzanne Mikesell
Cover Design: Hatley Mason

Prima Publishing & Communications
P.O. Box 1260JR
Rocklin, CA 95677
(916) 624-5718

Library of Congress Cataloging-in-Publication Data

Robinson, James W., 1954-

Winning Them Over

1. Public speaking. I. Title.

PN4121.R653 1987 808.5'1 86-22621

ISBN 0-914629-07-7

90 89 88 87 RRD 10 9 8 7 6 5 4 3 2 1

Printed in the United States of America by:
R.R. Donnelley & Sons Company

Acknowledgments

Some very special communicators have taught me, tested me, and challenged me: Peter Hannaford, Ronald Reagan, Jerry Solomon, Ken Khachigian, Dick Lesher, Don Kendall, George Deukmejian, and C.K. McClatchy.

Many others provided inspiration and assistance, among them: Lillian Brown, John Buckley, Misty Church, Ben Elliot, Kathleen Fitzgerald, Doug Gamble, Gary Holmes, Agnes Lesher, Steve Merksamer, Thang Quoc Pham, Gonejanart Rodbhajon, and Larry Thomas.

Finally, without the friendship, ideas, and skills of Ben Dominitz, Nancy Dominitz, and Suzanne Mikesell, there would be no *Winning Them Over*.

I thank you all.

Contents

A Tale of Two Executives

Bill Warner and John Harper have been buddies since grade school. They grew up in the same neighborhood. They soared to the top of their class in high school. When it came time for college, they earned the luxury of choosing from the best.

This story of mutual success continued through college and business school, where they were recruited by a number of companies on the lookout for promising executive material. Given their friendship, it was a fitting coincidence that both Bill and John signed up with the same firm.

But then they parted company.

It didn't take long for superiors to notice that Bill had something special that John lacked. John seemed ill at ease with co-workers. He shook visibly when making presentations. Once, when asked to report on his division's activities to the corporate brass, he appeared flustered, confused, and unprepared. The bosses lost interest and John lost his credibility.

The situation got worse. When the company sent John to testify at a legislative hearing regarding industrial pollution, the unfriendly questioners immediately put him on the defensive. They backed him into verbal corners, until he all but admitted that the company was not doing enough to protect the environment. Interviews with reporters following the hearing were even worse. The sessions ended with John muttering, "No comment, no comment," and scurrying away.

1

The front office spent the next day issuing denials and clarifications. One vice-president was overheard later telling his colleagues, "It's really too bad, because I know that John Harper is a bright, capable person. But if we want to put our best foot forward, we just can't depend on him. He may be a good behind-the-scenes guy. Keep him there."

It was different with Bill Warner. Bill not only knew the business but he also projected confidence and control. His briefings and reports before the company's top executives were always skillfully prepared and delivered in an appealing and persuasive style. Other employees in his division soon came to rely on Bill when they had a proposal to advocate or when their participation was sought at conferences, panels, and seminars.

Bill also seemed to understand the media in a way few of his peers could grasp. He was actually friends with some reporters! Whenever he was put forward as a spokesman, the stories always seemed to come out better.

That was ten years ago. Today, Bill is a senior vice-president and is being groomed by the Board of Directors as the next chief executive officer. John is assistant manager of one of the thirteen divisions now run by Bill.

The ability to communicate made the difference.

Before You Begin . . .

Define Your Communications Goals

You may think that an author who writes about dealing with the media, making speeches, and getting publicity presumes that the reader wants all the public attention he can get. I make no such assumption. For some executives, there are compelling reasons for aggressively seeking a high public profile. Others prefer a low profile and have no intention of becoming a fixture on the evening news.

If you fall into the latter category, you may be wondering why you need this book at all. My reply is this: Just because you don't intend to go knocking on the media's door doesn't mean the media and the public won't come knocking on yours. You need a communications strategy even if that strategy is to downplay public communications. If you want to give the media the "brush off," you have to know how to do it in a positive manner that protects your company from harm. Even a defensive approach, particularly when it comes to handling bad news, often requires aggressive tactics and deft dealings with the media.

What is the right public relations strategy for you and your organization? That question must be answered by you and your organization, based on your short- and long-term goals.

The place to begin is to perform a "communications audit." In a recently published business book, the authors recommend a soul-searching review of goals and strategies in the following nine areas.[1] I have noted the most likely purposes and benefits of effective communications in these areas.

1. **Employee communications** – Communicating effectively with employees — welcoming input, ideas, and complaints and becoming an admired and respected leader — can have a major impact on their morale, cooperation, and productivity.

2. **Industrial relations** – Only applicable to some companies, this area concerns the relationship between management and labor. Deftly communicating the company's offer and negotiating posture, whether hard-line or conciliatory, can have a crucial impact during union negotiations or strikes.

3. **Consumer public relations** – Different from advertising, consumer public relations describes the vast potential for marketing your products through free publicity in the news media.

One classic example of effective consumer public relations is the excitement created in the media for the debut of the Ford Mustang in 1964. Lee Iacocca describes the publicity coup:

> Four days before the car was officially launched, a hundred members of the press participated in a giant seventy-car Mustang rally from New York to Dearborn . . . .The Mustang was featured simultaneously on the covers of both *Time* and *Newsweek*. This was an outstanding publicity coup for a new commercial project. Both magazines sensed we had a winner, and their added publicity during the very week of the Mustang's introduction helped make their prediction a self-fulfilling prophecy. I'm convinced that *Time* and *Newsweek* alone led to the sale of an extra 100,000 cars. [2]

4. **Financial public relations** – Developing an effective program to increase the financial community's awareness and confidence in the company can have a profound effect on a company's growth and profitability and ability to attract investors. Raising the desirability and respectability of your company can raise the value of your stock. Privately held companies with a good profile and a trusted name may find that this image-making pays off in dollars and cents if and when they decide to go public.

5. **Community relations** – Companies inevitably impact the surrounding community in many ways, particularly economically and environmentally. Effectively communicating the organization's plans, for example, its expansion plans, to local political, governmental, and social leaders is essential. Community support can often

make the difference between a plan that proceeds and a plan that is blocked by concerted opposition.

6. **Government relations** – Laissez-faire capitalism has never existed in its pure, textbook form in our economy and it surely doesn't exist today. Government policies at all levels have an immeasurable impact on the economic climate in which your company is striving to succeed. A government relations program seeks to favorably influence the government's policies with respect to your company, and it seeks to resist those policies which could spell the difference between its life and death.

7. **Consumer affairs** – Keeping the customer satisfied is a simple, obvious rule. Maybe that's why it's broken so frequently! An effective consumer affairs strategy is one which welcomes customers' complaints and ideas and disseminates important consumer information.

In recent years, the nightmare of product tampering has tested a number of corporations in this area of communications. One source lauds the approach taken by Johnson & Johnson to shore up public confidence in Tylenol in the wake of several tampering-related deaths: "Johnson & Johnson recalled the capsules at a cost of $100 million and, in the process, moved the focus of the news coverage away from negative publicity and onto positive publicity about a corporation acting responsibly."[3]

Creative consumer affairs efforts also impacted consumer confidence in saccharin in the late 1970s. The artificial sweetener had been the subject of stories and studies linking it to cancer in mice, and there was a move to ban it completely. One source notes, "Hill & Knowlton [a leading public relations firm] came up with the idea that to equal the intake of saccharin that the Canadian mice were subject to, humans would have to drink 1,250 bottles of diet soda a day." That rationale "swept public consciousness in an era when studies were showing that virtually everything causes cancer."[4]

8. **Event publicity** – Related to consumer public relations, event publicity involves the staging of high-visibility functions to

introduce new products, dramatize new concerns, or announce major developments.

9. **Corporate advertising** – At its highest level, this field is already known for its sophistication in marketing, media production techniques, and even psychology. Its importance to publicizing consumer products is obvious. Yet, today, many advertising strategies involve conveying not just a product's merits but also its manufacturer's corporate values and philosophy. More and more, chief executives are becoming chief salespeople for their products and their organizations. You may wish, or be called upon, to do the same.

These nine areas of public relations demonstrate the range of circumstances in which your ability to communicate is vital. Just because you have no desire to become a "media darling," a "news source," or a frequently called upon banquet speaker doesn't mean you can neglect those skills that allow you to put your best foot forward or that distinguish you as a leader.

Your communications goals should be to promote yourself and your organization to your most critical audiences: employees, colleagues or superiors, customers, consumers and investors, government officials, community leaders, and news organizations. How well you communicate with some or all of these "publics" will determine your success or failure and that of your organization.

So, first determine which of the nine public relations areas are important to you and then define your goals:

- Do you want to increase sales by better publicizing your firm and its products?

- Do you want to garner greater respect among peers, superiors, and subordinates?

- Do you want to favorably influence public policy at the local, state, or national level?

- Do you want to create greater acceptance and a better public image for your organization in the community?

- Do you want to improve your company's financial base by increasing its visibility in the financial community?

- Do you want to be prepared when bad news strikes in order to avert negative publicity for your organization?

Only *you* can answer these questions. *Winning Them Over* answers this question: "Yes, but HOW DO I DO IT?"

You do it by becoming proficient in two challenging theaters of public performance: dealing with the media and delivering powerful speeches. While specific goals and audiences may differ from executive to executive, two constants remain:

1. You need the intermediaries of the media to tell your story — and that means you must know how to communicate through press releases, reporters, interviews, newspapers, radio, and television.

2. You need skillful, persuasive verbal powers — and that means you must know how to successfully communicate with your chosen audiences through speeches, presentations, panels, and other public appearances.

Hence, the two parts of this book: *Ten Strategies* for getting your message across through the media and *Ten Steps* to writing and delivering powerful speeches.

Make a Difference: Join the Communications Elite

The nation's top business leaders have become public figures to a remarkable extent:

- over 85% meet with outside groups

- 85% engage in public speaking

- nearly 50% lobby government agencies and officials

7

- nearly 70% engage in press conferences and media contacts

- 40% spend personal time on public issues

- 33% make television and radio appearances.[5]

The cream of the corporate crop have recognized the importance of communications to their companies, their country, and their careers. They know that the days of closeting themselves in the corner office to study balance sheets are over. Their organizations and their communities are looking to them for visible, active leadership. And even if they don't go looking for publicity, chances are publicity — and scrutiny — will come looking for them.

Some experts see these and other corporate and government executives as forming a new communications elite, "an increasingly powerful group with a potent blend of news and public relations talent," according to one source.[6] Wary of this new elite, they warn the news media to resist the influence of business and governmental "PR."

I don't share this mistrust. I believe the free market of ideas, vigorously advocated and imaginatively communicated — *and* hotly debated — is a positive development. My goal is to help *you* join the communications elite, to successfully get your message across through speeches, media contacts, and other public presentations.

Who Needs This Book?

When I told a fellow speechwriter and media consultant that I was going to write a book with these goals, he said, "Don't do it! You'll give away all our secrets!"

He wasn't joking.

Writing speeches and advising political, corporate, and community leaders on how to conduct themselves before the media is a lucrative business. Fortune 500 companies pay in excess of $100,000 a year for writers and communications professionals, and billing revenues at the fifty largest public relations companies now exceed $350 million.[7] Their value: helping chief executives and companies look good in front of a camera and win applause before selected audiences.

What if you have to talk to a reporter or make a speech and you don't have an extra $100,000 lying around? This book is for you. Consider it your personal speech consultant and your very own portable public relations department! More to the point:

- If you are the president of a small but growing company, your powers of persuasion are essential to its continued growth and your own personal success. This book is for you.

- If you are a division or branch manager looking forward to a bright future in your organization, you must do more than keep your eye on the bottom line. The boss's eye is on you. This book is for you.

- If you are a spokesman or information officer for a government agency or company, you will be called on daily to successfully deal with the media and tell your story boldly and confidently. This book is for you.

- If you are active in your church, union, political party, or trade association or if you are president of the PTA or the local Chamber of Commerce, you are a public figure. This book is for you, too.

- Most importantly, *if you want to rise higher in almost any field, to better serve your company or your organization, communications is the key. This book is for you.*

I have had the honor of writing speeches and providing media relations advice for some of the nation's top politicians and business executives. I have accumulated enough stories to last a lifetime. I draw upon these examples to illustrate key points. But I don't waste your time with a "look what I've done" ego trip. Nor do I spoonfeed you a glib "can-do" pep talk. Platitudes won't make you an effective communicator. Specific, practical, step-by-step, proven-to-be-successful advice will.

Communicating effectively is one part inspiration to three parts perspiration! It takes common sense and a lot of practice. Mine isn't the only system. There are others. But I have found one that works, one you can implement immediately without significantly disrupting your daily schedule. I'd like to share it with you. And don't worry, I promise we'll have fun along the way!

PART ONE

DEALING SUCCESSFULLY WITH THE MEDIA: TEN STRATEGIES

Part One: STRATEGY ONE

Make Peace with the Press

"A newspaper is the lowest thing there is!"

"It is well to remember that freedom through the press is the thing that comes first. Most of us probably feel we couldn't be free without newspapers, and that is the real reason we want newspapers to be free."

What if television had been around in the days of the Civil War? Pennsylvania State Senator Richard Snyder has already contemplated this fantasy (or nightmare) as he relates the following "transcript" of coverage of an important event:

DAN GATHER: We're here today at Gettysburg where President Lincoln is about to deliver an address. Aides admit it contains no news of the war . . . and little else, we expect. The president is being introduced now, so let's listen in . . .

ABE LINCOLN: Four score and seven years ago our forefathers brought forth . . .

GATHER: As we said, it looks as though the president is giving us a run-of-the-mill backgrounder. Nothing new up to now.

LINCOLN: We cannot hallow this ground. The brave men, living and dead, who struggled here . . .

GATHER: (Breaking in): I've been talking to our informed sources, and it seems worth pointing out that all are convinced that the president may be laying the foundation for his reelection campaign next year. Pennsylvania is a pivotal state, and coming to Gettysburg was essentially a political decision.

15

LINCOLN: We take increased devotion to that cause for which they gave that last full measure of devotion . . .

GATHER: Well, as I said, the president is not breaking new ground today, and as soon as he finishes . . . Yes, he's sitting down to, I must say, only polite applause. If President Lincoln expected to make history here today, I would say he has drawn a blank. Now, we switch to Richmond, Virginia, to get Jeff Davis' response . . . .[1]

Before you find yourself longing for those good old pre-television days, recognize that the press has played a key intermediary role in communicating information, news, and viewpoints since the days of the town crier. And news makers have been complaining about their coverage for just as long!

The first strategy for dealing successfully with the media doesn't cost any money, require any specialized skills, or even take a lot of time. But it does take discipline and self-control. The strategy is this: *Make peace with the press*.

If you're like me, you've been grumbling about what you've been reading in the paper and seeing on TV for as long as you can remember. We're not alone. By 1983, the National Opinion Research Center discovered that only 13.7% of the public had "a great deal of confidence in the press."[2]

I'm not one of those. I believe there are serious shortcomings in the way the American news media are doing their job.

I have met brilliant reporters who are tireless workers, original thinkers, and superb writers — individuals with the highest personal integrity. But for every one of those, I have met a reporter who is arrogant, cynical, negative, rude, lazy, and ideologically biased.

And I'm sure they feel the same way about me!

Nonetheless, whatever the shortcomings of some reporters, they do have a job to do, and it's an important job. Separate books have been and can be written to spur the media reforms I believe are necessary. But that is not my purpose here. My purpose is to convince you to do what I have done: Take note of your personal feelings about the press and file them away. Then, get on with the business of dealing with these important communications gate-keepers.

Like me, many executives and professionals are fearful, suspicious, and highly critical of the news media, and those feelings block good media relations. I am suggesting that without lying down to unfairness, you accept up front some basic facts of life about this institution. Rather than allowing the media's perceived shortcomings and your mistrust to paralyze your efforts at publicity, be prepared for a potential adversarial relationship and develop a strategy to understand it, control it, or change it.

With an Enemy Like the Press, Who Needs Friends?

Your relationship with the press will be a strange one, indeed! Except in rare cases, the press is not your enemy, and you are not theirs. How about adversary? This oft-used term describes a significant part of your media relationships. Most reporters consider it their duty to take a questioning stance and even "devil's advocate" approach vis-a-vis the representatives of society's institutions.

But adversaries normally don't need each other to do their jobs. You and the reporter *do* need each other. He needs you and many other sources in order to gather necessary information and to construct stories in a credible fashion. You need the reporter because he is the conveyor of your message to the public.

Adversaries who need each other. Adopt this conceptual framework and you are on your way to positive press.

The Never-Ending Question: Is the Press Biased?

Why does everyone love to knock the press? Perhaps it's because reporters are as human as you and I and just as unlikely to admit it.

17

Thankfully, American journalism has come a long way. In the eighteenth and early nineteenth centuries, American newspapers were often established mainly for promoting a particular political party's propaganda. Their attacks on opponents were downright scurrilous. They turned pioneer author James Fenimore Cooper into a pioneer of press libel suits. In the heat of his media battles he proclaimed, "If newspapers are useful in overthrowing tyrants, it is only to establish a tyranny of their own."[3]

Today, the press is much more professional. Even when journalists fall short, they still perform well above the standards of yesteryear.

Yet, the power of the American news media is vast. They represent the eyes and ears through which we experience the world and beyond. Like few other institutions, the media bind our diverse people into one nation with shared knowledge and experiences.

What we know of our nation's leaders we learn through the media. Except for a relatively small circle of friends and neighbors and the limited exposure of personal travel, what we know of our society and its people, we know because of the media.

This is enormous power. But we can take comfort in the fact that, in America, the news media are nearly as diverse as the people themselves.

There are over 9,000 commercial radio stations in America and more than 1,100 television stations. Nearly 10,000 newspapers are published. The daily papers alone have a combined circulation of more than 62 million copies a day. Another 10,000 periodicals, both general and specialized, are also published.

Yet, like any other large institution functioning in the free market of business and ideas, the press is led by its own trend-setters and opinion-makers. For example, three television networks (ABC, CBS, and NBC) and two major wire services (Associated Press and United Press International) ensure that every day tens of millions of people see, hear, and read the same accounts of major events.

Then there are the more subtle influences on the national news diet. Prestigious journalistic kingdoms like the *Washington Post*, the *New York Times*, and the *Wall Street Journal* often set the tone and the trends for coverage in other media. If these powerhouses decide that something is news, chances are other news organizations, particularly the three television networks, will as well. Why? Because television relies on print for much of its detail work.

When I lived in Washington, D.C., I read the *Washington Post* each morning. I then turned on one of the network morning news programs. I was often astounded at the similarity between the stories. Sometimes the television news copy would be nearly identical to the first few paragraphs of the *Post* story.

Former Senator Eugene McCarthy put it this way: "Journalists are like blackbirds on a telephone wire. One flies away and they all fly away. One comes back and they all come back."[4]

A most memorable example of the influence of the media trend-setters occurred in the presidential election of 1984. The first debate between President Ronald Reagan and former Vice-President Walter Mondale was widely judged a draw by the audience during and immediately following the debate.

Yet the president clearly had his bad moments — derailed trains of thought, unusually long hesitations, and confusing sentences. To long-time Reagan watchers, this was nothing new, but others' expectations were higher. After all, he was the "Great Communicator" — his opponent was supposed to be the lifeless and ineffectual one.

The editors of the *Wall Street Journal* decided that his performance may have been symptomatic of Reagan's advancing age. A front-page article two days after the debate carried the headline: "New Question in Race: Is Oldest U.S. President Showing His Age?"

That was all the other news media needed, particularly television. The networks trotted out earlier Reagan footage, such as a few drowsy moments with the pope in 1983. Doctors were interviewed. Specialists on senility were consulted. A once-taboo subject was fully opened up, much to the consternation of the Reagan campaign.

It is perhaps fitting, given the way a "pack journalism" mentality spawned this story, that in the end Reagan beat it back with an equally non-substantive one-liner. Was he too old to handle the rigors of the job? "Naw," Reagan deadpanned in the second debate. "I want you to know I will not make age an issue in this campaign. I am not going to exploit for political purposes my opponent's youth and inexperience."

In the words of political analysts Jack Germond and Jules Witcover, "All at once, for all practical purposes, the presidential election of 1984 was over."[5]

Given the power of a relatively small number of journalistic gatekeepers to set the tone and direction for much of the nation's news coverage, the question is frequently asked: Do these trendsetters as a group tilt in one particular direction on the political and philosophical spectrum? Journalists don't like this question because it bluntly challenges the central requirement of their profession — impartiality. Moreover, it begs and is often confused with a far more important question: If that personal bias exists, do most journalists successfully keep it out of their professional work?

I'm surprised there is any debate at all. While there *is* a healthy diversity of media throughout our country, media opinion-makers do, in general, inhabit the left side of the political spectrum.

Of the many studies of the press that have been conducted, one of the most frequently cited is that of S. Robert Lichter and Stanley Rothman. In 1981, they surveyed 240 leading journalists, along with middle- and upper-level news executives. Their conclusions are clear:

> We found that the media elite does have a more liberal and cosmopolitan social outlook than either business leaders or the general public. On economic issues, they are well to the left of businessmen. They are also suspicious of and hostile toward business, are far more critical of American institutions, and are much more sympathetic to the 'new morality' that developed in the 1960s.[6]

The survey draws this picture of the handful of people who decide what is news and how it will be portrayed:

- 95% are white
- 79% are male

- 93% are college graduates
- 46% earn over $50,000
- 54% say they are liberal
- 50% have no religion[7]

Lichter and Rothman surveyed journalists' voting patterns as well: 84% voted for President Johnson in 1964; 87% voted for Hubert Humphrey in 1968; and 81% voted for George McGovern in 1972 and Jimmy Carter in 1976.[8]

But what about tomorrow's media gatekeepers? In a follow-up study of journalism students at the prestigious Columbia School of Journalism, the authors discovered an even more pronounced tilt to the left. "Our findings show that these aspiring journalists are more liberal in attitude, more cosmopolitan in background, and more out of step with prevailing American beliefs than those already at the top of the profession."[9]

Eighty-five percent of journalism's next generation described themselves as politically liberal. While fifty-two percent of the American people voted for Ronald Reagan in 1980, just four percent of those journalism students did.[10]

There *are* some signs of healthy diversification of the media elite. Writing in the *New Republic*, columnist Fred Barnes concludes that, "Media realignment and the emergence of Reagan are signs of the same phenomenon: the conservative trend in American life."[11] Barnes points to developments such as the hiring of conservative George Will as ABC's evening news commentator and the births of the Cable News Network in 1980 and *USA Today* in 1982, which, he says, challenge the traditional liberalism of the New York/Washington news culture. Even so, Barnes concludes, "Reporters, especially those who cover national news, regard themselves as liberals."[12]

Another development has shaken the media establishment in recent years. As *U.S. News and World Report* summarizes, "Libel wars are being waged throughout the country as angry plaintiffs seek huge damages awards against the news media. This has put reporters and editors on the defensive and raised questions about the

21

accuracy and the ethics of the press."[13] Indeed, eighty-five percent of 106 major libel verdicts by juries since 1975 have resulted in defeats for the media defendants.[14]

What You Can Expect from Reporters

The issue of bias is more than just an interesting topic of discussion; it has deeply influenced many executives' approaches to the media. They review irrefutable evidence of reporters' negative attitudes toward business and they ask themselves, "Why should I bother?" They assume that reporters' antithetical views will color stories and damage their reputation and that of their organization. Accordingly, they take no positive actions to improve their coverage. Instead, to the extent that they deal with them at all, they carry out their contacts with the media in a context of belligerency, suspicion, and evasion.

Don't allow yourself to become one of these "unknown" professionals. Like you and me, reporters have every right to their personal opinions, even their own particular partisan affiliations. The issue of concern to communicators is: How well will reporters keep their personal opinions out of their stories? You won't succeed at changing and shouldn't try to change a reporter's basic philosophy; but with the right strategies, you can keep to a minimum the bias that may work its way into a story.

The majority of reporters attempt to approach their tasks with great professionalism. They struggle to be fair. However, I have concluded that more often than not, personal views and professional pressures, although not necessarily partisan ones, do influence the content and tone of stories in widely varying degrees.

Jody Powell, presidential press secretary during the Jimmy Carter administration, has experienced numerous frustrations dealing with imperfect reporters. He writes in his memoir, *The Other Side of the Story*:

The principal problem with journalism is not political or ideological bias . . . . The major bias in journalism, it seems to me, the one most likely to promote deception and dishonesty, has its roots in economics . . . .Members of the press wrestle with the most basic and pervasive of human motivations: greed and ambition.[15]

Washington Post reporter Lou Cannon observes:

The reporter's view that he is performing a sacred calling can cloak him with an amazing self-righteousness about his mission . . . .Out of this attitude of mission sometimes arises an insensitivity and a mistaken belief that the reporter is entitled to ask anyone anything at any time.[16]

The key to working successfully with these media gatekeepers is not your ability to change them, debate them, avoid them, or accuse them, but to understand what drives them and their profession. Here are basic qualities you can expect to see in many reporters:

Skepticism: Rather than overtly displaying political or ideological bias, reporters approach business and government with an attitude of skepticism and irreverence.

Journalists are trained to question everything they hear, to search for ulterior motives and back-room deals, to look beneath the surface, even if there is no "beneath the surface." You can expect very few of your statements to reporters to go unchecked or unchallenged.

Arrogance: Many reporters believe they are on a daily mission to ferret out what they consider the objective truth in a world where all viewpoints except theirs are subjective. If, for example, you are a corporate executive, everything you say or do is, in their view, colored by self-interest and the desire for self-promotion. Yet reporters are subject to no such flaws. They have the keenness of intellect and the moral rectitude to assess all competing versions of truth expressed by news makers and to determine for the public who is right and who is wrong.

If you analyze press coverage or propose reforms in the news-gathering process, you are "tampering with the First Amendment." If you are an important public official and you complain too loudly about a particular story, it will have "a chilling effect" on the free press. These and other rhetorical tactics are used by some journalists and their organizations to defend their profession's privileged status as a class of objective messengers of truth.

Strain: Reporters usually are under great pressure. Pressure to meet a deadline. Pressure to get the facts straight. In most cases, they will not be experts on the subjects at hand. They must educate themselves quickly and, in a matter of hours, write about the subject in comfortable, easily understandable terms. Then it's time to face the editor! (As a matter of fact, it sounds a lot like being a speechwriter.)

A corollary to this characteristic is *laziness*. Like any other field, journalism contains hard workers and, to be polite, not-so-hard workers. Combine the pressure of the deadline with a decided lack of gumption on the part of many reporters, and you see stories full of inaccuracies, oversimplification, and bad writing.

If you are the subject of such coverage and the coverage is critical in nature, this can be infuriating. As the veteran of a number of political campaigns, I can recall countless occasions when both my candidate and our opponent were victimized by reporters who simply repeated charges made by the other side without bothering to do the necessary homework to guide readers to an objective conclusion.

For example, in one race, the challenger accused the incumbent of "blocking seventeen efforts" to protect consumers. To my knowledge, not one reporter bothered to get a list of the supposed seventeen efforts in order to validate the charge. Nor did the opponent provide one. The press simply repeated the accusation, reporting only the general nature of the content of the blocked efforts.

For all the public knows, the incumbent may never have blocked any effort to help consumers. Or, he may have stopped thirty-four bills, not seventeen! Simply reporting the charge and writing stories focusing on "the horse race" aspect of the campaign was easier and more enjoyable for news writers than researching consumer legislation.

Competitiveness: Many reporters are greatly influenced by their peers. They fear missing a story that everyone else is writing about, yet at the same time they dream of discovering a story that no one else has found. Like other fields in today's economy, journalism is fiercely competitive. The view from the top is heady and exhilarating, but few make it to those altitudes.

Ambition: Visions of fame and fortune affect most of us — so too with reporters. In the aftermath of Watergate, journalism schools were flooded with would-be Woodwards and Bernsteins, all bent on uncovering the next great scandal. (The money is one thing, but to be portrayed in Hollywood by Robert Redford is quite another!)

But they haven't found it. They can't even come up with an original name for it. The surest indication is their insistence on labeling every minor business or government peccadillo with a word ending in the suffix "gate."

The resurgence of the muckraking strain in journalism is hailed by some like Leonard Downie, who writes in *The New Muckrakers*, "There would be no point in the press working to destroy society. Rather, it must help improve society, perhaps by helping to bring about significant changes. There is no reason, however, for the press to make any post-Watergate reconciliation with government by abandoning its present adversary posture."[17]

It may bring tears to Downie's eyes, but it appears that the aggressive muckrakers of the 1970s have mellowed. The present pursuit isn't solely for scandal but for professional respect and steady advancement in their organizations. Susan Miller of Scripps-Howard newspapers calls today's breed of reporters the "young and the restless." According to one editor, "There's no question they're much more concerned about a direct career ladder and moving up rapidly."[18]

The "Good News Is No News Syndrome": Along with skepticism, arrogance, strain, laziness, competitiveness, and ambition is a quality that infuriates news makers more than any other: obsessiveness with "bad" news. You have to do or say something bad, critical, or "off the wall" in order to make news. Many editors freely admit that novelty, dissension, or things going wrong have premium news value. Criticism, even negativism, sells more newspapers than praise and optimism.

Public relations executive and speechwriter Peter Hannaford has written that, "Because news, by its nature, is largely negative, the power these journalists wield is largely negative. They can tear down, but there is little they can build up."[19]

News makers must learn to live with this tendency, which, upon reflection, is not as galling as it first appears. Do we really expect to see stories with headlines such as: "Everything Being Properly Run at Amalgamated Steel?"

Expect Bias — Demand Fairness!

I suspect that most reporters would admit, to themselves if not to others, that bias-free reporting is impossible. Our journalistic institutions should end this facade and embrace a more realistic, achievable ethic — the ethic of fairness.

Though editors and reporters are loath to admit it, they are, as James J. Kilpatrick writes, mortal beings. "They are as mortal as appellate judges. Every reporter who covers the courts knows that judges do not take off their prejudices when they put on their robes. Judges bring to the bench the accumulated likes, dislikes, doubts, and convictions of a lifetime. So, too, with the men and women who decide what stories will make air tonight and what stories will be left out."[20]

Total objectivity may be impossible, but fairness is fundamental. An honest reporter should allow you to present your views and make your case right alongside opposing ones.

You and the Reporter May Have a Lot in Common

I'm not talking about your taste in clothes, food, or movies, but your goals as a professional, the pressures you face, and even your shortcomings!

- Like you, reporters bring to their task a lifetime of opinions, biases, and beliefs.

- Like you, they want to be successful. This may drive them to look for the story behind the story, ulterior motives, and even scandal.

- Like you, they are under considerable pressure to perform — to meet deadlines, to avoid factual errors, to write better and more newsworthy prose than their peers, and to keep their superiors happy.

- Like you, most take their craft seriously. If they feel no loyalty to their papers, they certainly do to their profession. When they fall short in accuracy or fairness, it is usually unintentionally.

- *Unlike* you, they may be totally unfamiliar with the subject at hand when covering you or your organization. It is your job and opportunity to educate them — to become not just an object of nagging inquiry but a frequently quoted, authoritative resource.

How do you do that? Turn the page!

Get Out of Your Bunker

"The old nobility would have survived if they had known enough to become masters of printed materials."

Napoleon Bonaparte

If you and your organization have completed the public relations audit recommended earlier, you have reached some decisions about your goals in dealing with the media. Perhaps you want to join a growing number of executives who want a high public profile for themselves and their companies. Or, perhaps you don't desire media coverage, but your position in the community and the economy prompts reporters to call on you anyway.

Either way, you need some basic strategies to improve your press coverage and protect your organization's relationship with the public as it is presented through the media.

As we discussed, the first strategy is to make a concerted effort to *understand* the media. Learn some basic facts and spot some general trends among journalists so that you are prepared to take what they are eager to dish out. Unless you have chosen a career as a media watchdog or reformer, accept the media for what it is — an imperfect yet indispensable link between the people and society's decision-makers in all fields.

But acceptance of journalism's status quo does not mean you should be passive. Many of you likely pride yourselves on your sales strategies and ability to market. I'm suggesting that you do not fall silent when it comes to marketing your organization and what it stands for in the media. Join the fray in the free market of ideas and opinions.

If you want to make a difference in the quality, if not the quantity of your press coverage, adapt an aggressive, proactive media approach, one that entails not only responding to reporters' questions but resourcefully seeking varied opportunities to tell your story. The alternative? A defensive duck, run, and hide strategy which I call:

The Bunker Mentality

No, I'm not talking about the Archie Bunker mentality but the losing general's bunker mentality. Many organizations, executives, and professionals hold attitudes like these:

"The press is out to get us. They always look for the dark cloud in the silver lining."

"Let's not tell the press anything. They'll just twist it and distort it."

"I can't stand these reporters. They don't know anything about business. We'll never get a fair shake no matter what they do. I'm just not going to deal with them."

Do any of these sentiments sound familiar? Many men and women in positions of responsibility and potentially high visibility are hiding in their bunkers, fussing and fuming about their press coverage but failing to do anything constructive about it.

This helps explain the often unfriendly relationship between the business community and the press. Both sides bear some blame, but it's the public that suffers. People are denied a full-bodied explanation of business and economic issues. That leads to misunderstanding. The ensuing antagonistic arguments generate mistrust among the public about both institutions: the press and business.

In Strategy One, we focused on some of the shortcomings of the news media and discussed certain habits among reporters which are partly responsible for this antagonism. Now, it's time to turn our sights to the business and professional communities.

The Lichter-Rothman study reported that "media and business leaders view each other with mutual suspicion, if not outright hostility. Each group rates the other as the most influential group in

32

America; moreover, each wants to reduce substantially the power of the other and to take its place as the most influential group."[1]

Former reporter and now public relations executive Dorothy Lorant has had ample experience to confirm this conclusion:

"A serious rift exists between the press and the private sector today, reinforced by businessmen who frequently approach an interview with a newspaper or television reporter with all the enthusiasm of a missionary asked to dine with cannibals," she writes. "Until each understands the other's role and function and begins to report the differences, they will continue to glower at each other with part suspicion and part monumental ignorance."[2]

Lorant has discovered that for every reporter guilty of bias, there is also a businessman "loathe to face up to any unpleasantness and who has a penchant for understating and obscuring bad news about his company."[3]

A case in point. In 1981, a Delta Airlines plane bound for Tampa, Florida, made what must have seemed to the passengers a routine and uneventful landing. Except for one problem — the plane landed at the wrong airport, an Air Force base eight miles away. Delta refused to comment. This did not diminish the coverage in any way — it increased it.

Worse than no comment is a response that is just not true. Commenting on the common belief in business circles that even *Wall Street Journal* reporters are suspicious of corporate America, an unidentified public relations director once said, "The *Wall Street Journal* may seem to have an anti-business bias, but if you had been lied to by as many business people as most *Journal* reporters have, you would be skeptical about business, too."[4]

In order to receive favorable press, you have to say something and you have to tell the truth. Silence is not golden, it's yellow. To reporters trained in the art of raising the eyebrow, it's an indication that you have something to hide. It only makes the reporter want to dig deeper.

Where does the reporter dig? Lorant properly warns us that he or she talks to competitors and/or disgruntled employees — people who don't know the full story and who are least inclined to say nice things about you. The story will still get written, and it will more likely read the way you had originally feared — one-sidedly.[5]

Jody Powell confirms this: "As the old saying goes, when in doubt, get it out. No matter how smelly it seems to be at first, it always gets worse as it ages."[6]

One simple suggestion: Relax! Lower your tension level about media coverage. Not every word can be flattering. Lorant comments: "Most businessmen do not understand that a story is not bad simply because every word is not complimentary. Executives often brood over a nuance here, a critical observation there, complaining that the reporter is 'hostile' for having raised an unwelcome or controversial perspective."[7]

I recall a leading business executive's reaction to a lengthy profile appearing in a nationwide publication. The article was glowing — not because it rehashed company boilerplate about the executive, but because it told the story, warts and all, of a determined man who rose from nowhere to successfully lead a giant conglomerate. Any fair reader would finish the story with a sense of admiration and even awe.

One of the awe-inspiring details in the story concerned the executive's stupendous salary, bonuses, and perks. There it was, in black and white, on page thirty-two, close to the end of the story. The businessman was furious. He didn't want such information out. He had refused to detail his compensation, and so the reporter had tapped other sources. "He didn't explain it right," fumed the executive. "He had no right. It's personal. I'm going to get to the bottom of how he found out!"

On what should have been a glorious day for him and the company, he was discussing "cutting off" a reporter who had written an overwhelmingly positive story!

Since our goal is positive press, you won't find me trying to convince you to gratefully accept critical coverage. And, in Strategy Nine, I will suggest when, and when not, to complain. Yet, understand that your depiction of reality may not be shared by reporters. Your standard should be: Is the article fair to me? Does it convey to otherwise uninformed readers a good impression or a bad one? Will the resulting publicity help me and my organization or create problems I don't need?

These common-sense standards could make some would-be news makers recoil. Executives are accustomed to being in control. They like it. Who doesn't? To let someone else tell your story, someone who is not on your payroll and who may not even respect what you're doing, is to dangerously relinquish control.

That's true, *if* you stay hidden in that bunker. But if you take the initiative, even if that means taking some risks, you can have a dramatic effect on the quantity and quality of your media coverage.

You Need the Press — And the Press Needs You

Some businessmen have witnessed their colleagues learning this important lesson. According to General Foods Chairman Philip Smith, "Many business leaders are more willing than ever before to sit for interviews for print or broadcast. Likewise in the press, there is what appears to be an increased willingness by those on the editorial side to understand how business works."[8]

The hard truth is that if you want to be an effective communicator and a successful leader, you need the media's help. The press can publicize you, your activities, your products, and your organization. They can help establish your business reputation and your public notoriety. We see much of our world through the media. When you appear in those media in a favorable light on a frequent basis, you become an important "somebody" to colleagues, superiors, and strangers in a confusing, crowded, and competitive world.

Don't squander these opportunities. Let the media, once your adversaries, help you and your organization to a successful future.

Make Reporters Call on You

"Journalism: A profession whose business is to explain to others what it personally does not understand."

Lord Northcliffe

In Strategies One and Two, we focused primarily on changes in your mental attitude which are essential to gaining effective media coverage. Understanding some basic facts about the journalism profession and the habits of reporters is fundamental to making a good impression (Strategy One). So is a decision on your part to aggressively pursue media contacts and coverage rather than avoid them (Strategy Two).

The payoff can be substantial. According to some estimates, nearly half of the stories in a newspaper were initiated by a press release or by contacts from the business, political, governmental, and public relations professionals. In the case of the *Wall Street Journal*, one editor reports that about ninety percent of the daily coverage is prompted by companies making their own announcements and pronouncements.[1]

A leading network television executive describes a similar situation in that medium. "Quite a few of our story ideas come from PR people. All three of our programs, *20/20, Nightline*, and *World News Tonight*, use them."[2]

Local television news and talk shows, with many more hours of air time to fill, also depend heavily on ideas and stories not ferreted out by investigative reporters but brought to their attention by the news makers themselves.

Your opportunities are endless. What is the news? If you follow the strategies in this book, the news, to a great degree, can be what *you* make it, and it can be told the way *you* write it.

The Media Survey

The first step is to determine which media you want to reach and which media want to reach you so that you can build bridges of contact and communication.

Begin by conducting a media survey. Create a file on your computer or use a three-ring notebook. Make an entry for each news organization in your domain. Compile lists of key personnel in each newsroom, along with current phone numbers. Keep notes of calls and conversations. Save clippings which indicate reporters' specialties as well as their likes and dislikes.

Kept current, your media survey will quickly become your handy "bible," full of details about the reporters and news organizations who can help determine your future by the manner in which they present you to the public.

To better understand how to compile a media survey and how to make it work for you, let's consider the example of a fictional communicator at work.

Cindy Smoothtalker is branch manager for a large electronics firm, and she happens to be one of the first women to achieve this level in her company. The future looks bright. Who knows where this achievement will lead? To future promotions in business? Opportunities in politics and public office?

As a leading employer, Cindy's branch is an important establishment in the community. She is a natural focus for media attention, and she has decided to take the initiative. Equally important, she knows that the extent to which she can skillfully field media inquiries will be closely watched by the corporate brass. Her success or lack of it could determine her rate of advancement in the ranks.

Cindy begins by identifying all the news organizations in her geographical and subject area she would like to reach, or which she knows would like to reach her — including newspapers, television stations, radio stations, business publications like the Chamber of Commerce newsletter, and trade and community periodicals.

Setting priorities is important, too. Given the multitude of news media today, you should identify for the greatest personal attention those key outlets which will most likely cover you on a regular basis. Devote your scarce time to the media which could have the most impact on you and your activities, even if such media are local and seem to be less important than national news outlets.

For example, the business reporter for your home-town newspaper will likely be covering every decision and action you make, whereas the *Wall Street Journal* may cover your activities rarely or not at all. The *Journal*, while more significant nationally, in this example is less critical than the local papers. Also, it is far more realistic to expect a direct relationship with the local newspaper.

Don't neglect statewide or national media, particularly the wire services, Associated Press and United Press International, whose assigned reporters cover your geographic area. Send them press releases and cultivate contacts, but only after you have set priorities as to which outlets are most important to *you*.

Upon completing this step, Cindy Smoothtalker compiles some essential information on key personnel. Cindy will want to know the business editor and business reporters who cover her company's activities for the newspaper. She also wants to know about reporters who specialize in environmental issues, often a touchy subject for manufacturing concerns.

As one of the most successful businesswomen in the community, she could be an excellent subject for a profile in the "features" or "lifestyles" section. She should know these writers as well.

For stories and coverage of a more general nature, contact with the city editor is crucial. Finally, in order to develop input into the paper's editorial policies, she should not fail to recognize the role of the editorial page editor.

How does Cindy find out who these individuals are? Simple observation is one method. The paper publishes a limited masthead on weekdays which lists key personnel. On Sundays, the list is more detailed and extensive. She also examines by-lines closely and determines who is assigned to which kinds of stories. She notes these assignments in her media survey.

For television and radio, she compiles similar information but confronts some important differences. The news staff is smaller and

The Sacramento Bee

McCLATCHY NEWSPAPERS
Owner and Publisher
Published Daily and Sunday and twice on Wednesday.
Member of the Associated Press
The Associated Press is exclusively entitled to the use for publication of all news published herein

THE SACRAMENTO BEE	McCLATCHY NEWSPAPERS
C.K. McCLATCHY .... Editor	JAMES McCLATCHY .... Chairman of the Board
GREGORY E. FAVRE .... Executive Editor	C.K McCLATCHY .... Editor, President
FRANCIS KRAMNIC ..... Assistant Managing Editor	ERWIN POTTS .... Executive Vice President
ED CANALE .... Assistant Managing Editor	ROBERT BYERLY .... Director of Operations
JAMES DAWSON .... Assistant Managing Editor	O.J. BRIGHTWELL .... Assistant to Vice President
GEORGE L. BAKER .... Metropolitan Editor	
MIKE D. FLANAGAN .... City Editor	★ ★ ★
LORETTA NOFFSINGER Superior California Editor	
MORT SALTZMAN .... Executive News Editor	PETER SCHRAG .... Editorial Page Editor
KAREN J. SMITH .... News Editor	WILLIAM MOORE .... Forum Editor
WILLIAM F. ENDICOTT ..... Capitol Bureau Chief	JAMES J. BROWN .... Associate Editor
RALPH FRATTURA .... Features Editor	RHEA WILSON .... Associate Editor
DAVID JENSEN .... Executive Business Editor	ROBERT MOTT .... Associate Editor
STAN JOHNSTON .... Executive Sports Editor	
GEORGE WEDDING ..... Director of Photography	
BILL ALLEN .... Night Editor	OFFICE
PAUL CLEGG .... Head of Copy Desk	Sacramento Bee
★ ★ ★	Twenty First and Q
	Sacramento, CA 95816
FRANK R. J.WHITTAKER ...... General Manager	Telephone (916) 321-1000
FULLER A. COWELL .... Operations Director	REPRESENTED NATIONALLY BY
GARY E. MURRAY .... Finance Director	CRESMER, WOODWARD,
GENE H. GRANT .... Advertising Director	O'MARA & ORMSBEE
EUGENE A. CZARNY ...... Circulation Director	Member of the Audit Bureau of Circulation
DENISE L. LONGWOOD .... Personnel Director	Second class postage paid at Sacramento, California
OWEN SMITH ..... Plant and Production Director	
ELLEN L. SNODGRASS ...... Marketing Director	

SUBSCRIPTION RATES BY MAIL

In California, Nevada and Oregon Daily & Sunday $9.50 per month, $114.00 per year; Sunday-only $6.00 per month, $72.00 per year. In other states daily & Sunday, $10.50 per month, $126.00 per year; Sunday only $6.50 per month, $78.00 per year. Mail subscriptions are payable in advance. The Sacramento Bee Food Plus Issue, $5.20 annually. inclusive in all mail. Daily and Sunday and Sunday only subscriber rates.

(USPS 474-760) 42,883

Most newspapers print a roster of key news and editorial personnel.

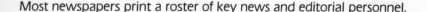

less specialized. She focuses her attention on the news director, the assignment editor, and the editorial director as the gatekeepers who decide which stories their reporters and camera crews cover. Some of this information rolls by on the screen after the news broadcast. Other details are ascertained simply by calling the newsroom and asking.

There are also a number of useful media guides, which can be found in any good library. After reviewing several of these publications, you might even decide to subscribe to the ones that fit your needs best. Because the information changes frequently, most are updated regularly. The following is just a sampling of many:

Working Press of the Nation
Ayer Directory of Publications
Bacon's Publicity Checker
Editor and Publisher International Yearbook
Broadcasting Yearbook
Hudson's Washington News Media Contacts Directory
Television Contacts
Radio Contacts
Standard Rate & Data Service
TV Publicity Outlets Nationwide
National Radio Publicity Outlets[3]

Cindy's goal is your goal as well. Determine who is or should be covering you and your activities. Once you have identified the media in your domain, begin establishing contacts and developing relationships. Make yourself known to the press. Become a resource rather than just a target. As one source stresses, "There is just no substitute for direct and frequent contact with news people as a means of improving your press relations."[4]

"Pleased to Meet You" — The Soft Sell

After you have surveyed the territory, start contacting the key people in your priority news organizations on a systematic basis. You don't need to meet all the appropriate editors and reporters immediately, but, at the very least, you should introduce yourself to one key contact in each newsroom. Find out when the newsroom's deadline for stories is and to whom you should direct press releases and other information. This could be the business editor, political editor, city editor, or a specific reporter, depending on your field and the nature of the news organization.

As you make your initial rounds, don't overdo it with a breathless sales pitch about your sterling qualities and the countless virtues of your company. Rather, simply introduce yourself by phone or in a brief meeting. Explain in a businesslike fashion your position or assignment, and ask to whom you should be directing press releases and other materials regarding your organization.

For example, suppose we were to listen in on a conversation between Cindy Smoothtalker and the business editor of the *Hometown Press* shortly after she assumed her new position:

Cindy Smoothtalker: Hello, Mr. Business Editor, my name is Cindy Smoothtalker. I was recently named branch manager for Universal Electric here in Hometown.

Business Editor: Oh, yes, we ran a story about your promotion. Congratulations. What can I do for you?

Cindy Smoothtalker: I know you are busy but I wanted to call and introduce myself and ask where we should be directing press releases and the like. I know the paper is on our mailing list but I want to be sure the information is getting to the right people on time.

Business Editor: We see some material from time to time, but I'm not sure I'm getting it all. I notice you're sending it to the city desk. Sometimes they ship it over to me. Sometimes it just gets tossed. I suggest you send a second copy directly to John Acidpen. He's our new general business reporter. And if you have a major announcement to make, I think you should have someone drop it off at our front desk. Our deadline is 4:00 PM, and it's Friday noon for the Sunday section.

Cindy Smoothtalker: Thank you very much. I hope we have a chance to meet soon. I'd like to tell you about some of our plans over here.

Business Editor: Sounds good. Call when you're settled and we'll set something up.

When I was working as a public relations executive on behalf of the Republic of China (Taiwan), I was responsible for acquainting

44

United States editorial staffs with the concerns and issues involving China and Taiwan.

One week every month, I identified a state or region to cover and called the editorial page editors of daily newspapers. I introduced myself and my client. I said that I planned to be in town on a particular date and that I would appreciate the opportunity to stop by for several minutes to meet the editor and to provide him with some materials about Taiwan.

In all but a few cases, my calls met with cooperation and success. Most times, I was able to meet with the editorial page editor; in other instances, I met a designated writer. As busy as they were, these press representatives felt a responsibility to meet with me.

I tried not to abuse this courtesy. I took just a few minutes to briefly review the activities and concerns of Taiwan, provide some reference information, and then question the editor as to whom to direct press releases and newsletters.

When I returned from my visits, I wrote short thank-you notes to each person I met. In some cases, I never saw or talked to the individuals again. In others, they became valuable links to the news media and even personal friends.

I learned one other lesson on these forays. While I was able to obtain meetings with newsroom personnel, meetings which were almost always friendly and positive, my visits won far more interest when I brought a representative from the Taiwan government with me.

Many journalists place a premium on companies and organizations whose principal executives are directly and readily available. Reporters are growing tired of spending time with intermediaries such as public relations "handlers," and some papers have even adopted policies against such contacts.

Hence, we have uncovered another advantage of the "do-it-yourself" approach to media relations which I am outlining in this book. Doing it yourself will not only save you money but it may win you more credibility than if you did have that large public relations department. You are your own best salesperson and, in the view of many reporters, nothing beats the real thing!

45

Don't Neglect TV and Radio Contact!

Local television may employ reporters of tremendous talent, intelligence, and expertise, but it provides less in-depth coverage than local papers do. Its tendency toward generalities is great. Television's pictures may be worth the proverbial thousand words, but the typical front page of a newspaper likely contains more copy than an entire TV news broadcast. Television reporters can't rely solely on the phone for researching and interviewing. They need pictures. Therefore, they must commit greater resources (e.g. camera crews) to each story than newspapers do.

The gatekeeper at a television station is the news director or assignment editor. He or she makes the crucial decisions as to how to allocate the station's handful of reporters and crews each day.

Call to determine who these people are, then introduce yourself with an even softer sell than you used for newspapers. The key focus of these calls should be informational: To whom do I send materials and press announcements about my organization's activities? Maybe this inquiry will trigger a deeper conversation. Maybe it won't. I have found television news editors more abrupt than newspaper personnel — perhaps because they face greater demands on their time while having fewer available resources.

Yet despite these limitations, television news often displays some unusual quirks. In April, 1986, fifteen members of the California National Guard volunteered to participate in a road-building exercise in Honduras. Even though the training was humanitarian in nature and occurred over one hundred miles from the Nicaraguan border, some brilliant news editor decided that their participation had deep international significance. This was California "intervening" in an impending "war" in Central America.

No less than five local television stations decided to send TV crews and reporters down to Honduras to report on, as one station hyped it, "The California Connection." Reporters donned their designer khakis, studied their maps of Central America (probably for the first time since grade school), and rode many hours on military transports. The reports were thrilling — if you like watching asphalt poured onto a dirt road!

No telling how many important stories went uncovered during this "expedition." Perhaps your important story was one of them. This is the marketplace in which you are competing. Press attention, particularly television, is a scarce commodity, and you must constantly sell the newsworthiness of your story. It helps if you can develop a relationship with the buyers.

Don't make the mistake of forgetting radio. It is a news source for millions. In small communities, the local radio station can be as popular as the local newspaper — particularly if its programming includes a good talk show. In larger communities, radio benefits from the captive audience of commuters. Think about it — workers trapped in freeway traffic may as well be listening to good news about your organization.

Become a Media Resource

If you think that you can make news only when you do something newsworthy, you may never see your name in print or know the alluring glare of the TV lights. Change your thinking. News is what you can convince the editors and reporters that it is. When you say or do something you would like covered, you have to know whom to contact to invite their coverage. You will be competing for attention with dozens of other would-be news makers.

Whether or not you succeed depends on the resources of the news organization as well as the editor's opinions of your activities. But it also depends on whether or not you are known and respected in the newsroom and how well you make your case. "Top executives who become known for well-spoken remarks and polished delivery," experts have concluded, "are more likely to be sought for comment, particularly by broadcast journalists."[5]

Many media inquiries will come naturally, a reflection of your prominence or the prominence of your organization. Sometimes the calls will pertain to sensitive subjects or even result in potentially "bad" news for the company. Your goal in these instances is to make your organization's case in a clear and convincing fashion and to have your position featured fairly and prominently in the news story.

Even if your public relations plan calls for adeptly handling unsolicited media inquiries rather than seeking publicity and a high profile, your efforts will be aided immeasurably if you know the reporters and editors with whom you are dealing and if they know you. If a foundation of confidence and communication has already been built, your chances of success will be greatly improved.

For those who want more, who want to be a visible player on the media's stage, the objective is different. When a story calls for a comment by someone in your field or for an example of someone in your situation, will the reporter think to call you first? That should be your goal.

Dealing effectively with the media requires reciprocity. You must not only be prepared for the inquiring phone call. You should, through your promotional activities, *make news*. You should, through the media relationships you develop, *make those phone calls happen*.

How? We'll discuss promotional activities in Strategy Eight. As for media relationships, it is important that you gain a reputation for providing usable, accurate information. Be counted on as a place to go for a good, lively quote or even some inside information. But learn to separate real news from non-news. Don't flood reporters with an endless stream of frivolous press releases and bothersome phone calls. According to one expert, "Building a reputation as the source of adequate, factual, and timely information for the news media depends on one's own ability to distinguish non-news from news and to keep the former to oneself."[6]

Obviously, reciprocity does not mean currying favor with the press by saying things that deliberately undercut your company or other members of the team. Such disloyalty is not worth the price. Be helpful without fawning. Be honest without talking "out of school."

Can you trace the precise course by which you have developed all your salient friendships and professional relationships? You may recall the first meeting and perhaps a project or common interest that sparked the connection. But who's to say exactly how or why certain people become personally or professionally close to each other? The same goes for your relationships with the news media. There is no sure-fire formula.

Rest assured, however, that you don't have to go out drinking with the folks in the newsroom to get good press. You *do* have to be sensitive to their needs and interests and be receptive to developing mutually beneficial professional relationships.

Most human relationships are developed on the basis of mutual need. You need reporters and they need you. Your media contacts are critical to you. Reporters' contacts are critical to them.

Behind every edition of the daily paper and every news broadcast is what has been, up to now, an alien world for most professionals. Peel the veil of unfamiliarity from these organizations. Follow the simple course outlined in this strategy and become familiar with that unknown world.

For many years, I was shy and even fearful of talking to reporters. I was uncomfortable in the belief that they were constantly judging me and looking for grounds on which to criticize me.

I'm still on guard, and I find conversations or lunches with reporters much less enjoyable than, say, those with colleagues. That's because you always have to watch what you say — even if the reporter has loosened you up with friendly talk and good company.

Yet, when you go into these situations with knowledge of the reporter's habits, style, and professional pressures, you've accomplished a large part of the task of dealing with the media in a confident and effective manner.

But you're not ready yet. Before sitting down with a reporter, you must clearly define exactly what it is you hope to accomplish in the meeting. Turn the page.

Before the Interview: Plan Your Answers in Advance

"Journalism is literature in a hurry."

Matthew Arnold

The interview — a give-and-take between a reporter and a news maker — is a fundamental news-making ritual. Whether it is a full-blown press conference with twenty reporters firing questions, an informal telephone conversation, or a one-on-one meeting with a journalist, a few crucial preparations can make you a winner.

Let's explore these preparations from start to finish by rejoining Cindy Smoothtalker, who is about to be grilled on how her company disposes of toxic waste — a hot topic for any manufacturing executive!

The Saga of John Acidpen and Cindy Smoothtalker

The Facts: The federal Environmental Protection Agency has just issued a report declaring that community water supplies all over the country are potentially contaminated because of antiquated, inadequate, and sometimes even illegal toxic chemical disposal. Cindy heads a branch of an electronics firm that is located in one of the communities named in the report.

The phone rings: Cindy's secretary tells her that John Acidpen of the *Hometown Herald* is calling. Knowing from her media survey that this reporter specializes in environmental and public health issues, she decides that she wants to do a little investigating before she takes the call. She asks her secretary to inform John that she is "in a meeting" and will get right back to him.

Next, Cindy makes some calls to key people at the home office to see if they know what John Acidpen might be up to. Through them, she learns that EPA has issued a report an hour ago and that, yes, it includes Hometown as one community in which unusually high traces of certain toxics were found in the ground water. That's probably why he's calling.

She realizes that any company response is going to require some research and strategy, but she also wants to get back to John as soon as possible. Cindy calls him back:

Cindy Smoothtalker: Hello, John, I wanted to get back to you as soon as possible. What can I do for you?

John Acidpen: If possible, I'd like to come over and ask you a few questions.

Cindy: May I ask what it's regarding?

John: Sure. Are you aware that EPA has issued a report today naming Hometown as a toxic-contaminated community? I'd like to know how your company plans to explain to the residents that their water may be poisoned because of the chemicals you use in your manufacturing process.

Cindy: Yes, we're aware of the report, but we haven't had a chance to review it. After we have had that opportunity, I'd be happy to talk with you on the record. What's your deadline?

John: It's five PM. So if you want a comment in the story, I really need to see you no later than four.

Cindy: You've got it. Come over at four.

John: Thanks. See you then.

After setting up the interview, prompt enough to meet John's deadline but far away enough to prepare, Cindy goes to work. She obtains a copy of the report, studies its findings, and searches for specific references to Hometown and the company. She refreshes her memory about the company's other activities in the waste disposal area. She consults with company headquarters to determine the latitude she will be allowed in acting and responding. Most importantly, *she decides what she wants to say before the interview begins.*

How can Cindy do that when she doesn't even know what the questions are? If she has done her homework properly, she should be able to anticipate nearly every question. Even if she misses a couple, she has already devised the message she wants to impart. Nothing, but nothing, will deter her from that message.

Questions anticipated, answers determined, message devised, homework done, Cindy is ready at four for her meeting with John Acidpen.

He arrives on time. She shows him in right away . . . .

Stop the Presses!

Before continuing with this saga, let's take a moment to review Cindy's preparation strategies:

- Rather than taking John's call right away, she stalled for just enough time to do some quick digging as to why he might be calling. This approach should be used only when necessary. In this case, *it enhanced Cindy's credibility* because instead of having to be told by John about the report, she already knew about it by the time they talked. Nevertheless, *she followed the critical rule of promptly returning a reporter's call.*

- Because she had already taken the time to survey the local media, *Cindy already knew who John was,* his area of expertise, his personal opinions, and the topics of his recent articles. This information proved valuable at a later stage.

- When Cindy returned John's call, *she was not defensive or suspicious,* but confident, cheerful, and willing to cooperate.

- *Cindy did not hesitate to ask John about the purpose of his inquiry.* You should never hesitate to do this either. Call it the public's right to know!

- *Cindy was sensitive to both John's need to meet his deadline and the company's need to plan and prepare its response.* Hence, the late afternoon interview. Cindy wisely refused to be pushed into an interview before she was fully prepared.

- Let's not overlook the fact that *she agreed to the interview*, reflecting her wise strategy of being forthright and responsive, even when faced with a possibly negative story. Note that John clearly implied that 1) his story would be written whether Cindy commented or not and 2) he had already decided on a somewhat negative lead — namely, that industries such as hers were to blame for toxic contamination of the local water supply.

- By saying she would respond "on the record," *Cindy clearly established the ground rules* for the interview — although in this case, she really didn't need to. Why? Because unless you specify differently, everything you say to a reporter can be quoted by name.

Here are the commonly accepted interview rules when dealing with reporters:

On the record: Everything you say can be used, and you can be quoted by name.

Not for attribution and **On background**: You can be quoted but not directly identified. You may be described in such phrases as "a top company official" or "an aide close to Congressman Jones."

On deep background: Whatever the reporter uses cannot be linked to you at all but must be asserted on the journalist's own authority.

Off the record: The material cannot be used in any form except to guide the reporter's thinking. This agreement is sometimes broken if a story becomes public or if the journalist finds other sources who will attest to it.

- Using the time in between the phone call and the interview, *our communicator boned up on company policies*, familiarized herself with the EPA report, and consulted company superiors and experts. Knowing the facts is critical to a successful interview.

- Finally, *Cindy anticipated the questions* John would ask, *planned the answers*, and *determined the basic message* she hoped to communicate to the public via the press. She did not forget that her true audience is the public, not the press. She readied herself for the interview, knowing exactly what she wanted to convey, and she was determined not to be deterred from that goal.

I suggest that novice news makers go one step further. It is very helpful to actually write out in advance anticipated questions and your responses. This exercise helps you crystallize your thoughts, particularly your reactions to the tough, negative questions. It focuses your attention on the "style" of your answers as well as their substance. It prompts you to explain yourself in the most compelling, persuasive, and even entertaining manner.

Don't cheat when writing out an interview scenario in advance. Pose the toughest possible questions. Be prepared for the worst, and you may be pleasantly surprised if half of those questions never arise. That beats not being prepared for a "zinger" and finding yourself reduced to a stuttering fool!

To some members of the press, anticipating questions and planning answers smacks of packaging. They suggest that if you have to think about your answer and dress it up, you must have something to hide. They believe the spontaneous answer is more truthful.

I disagree. There is nothing wrong with thinking and planning. There is nothing wrong with deliberation. Communicating effectively with the public takes preparation, and that's the goal of the news maker — to communicate with the public through the news media. Of course, you also want to look and sound good along the way. Who doesn't?

Larry Thomas, press secretary to California's Governor George Deukmejian, comments on his preparation for gubernatorial news conferences: "Our process isn't very elaborate. We solicit input from agency secretaries and department heads on issues they think might come up. A synopsis of these reports is given to the governor. Judging by the nature of reporters' questions, we are pretty close in predicting the issues that are raised in the press conference."

My colleague is being diplomatic by understating the degree to which preparation works in California. I have found it easier to predict questions asked by the California press corps at a general news conference than it is to guess students' questions when the governor visits a grade school assembly.

I do not mean to insult the press but rather to support the view that, for the most part, reporters aren't out to throw you off balance with off-the-wall questions. They have a job to do. They're covering the critical issues of the day for their readers in a logical, methodical fashion.

The press can benefit from your advance preparation as well. The less prepared a cautious or scared news maker is, the less likely he is to be truly responsive and informative.

When Not to Do an Interview

Is accepting an interview request always the right thing to do? What about those occasions when the news is bad — or worse, when you are convinced that the reporter is out to do a hatchet job on you?

Analyzing the situation is essential. If your company's over-the-counter drug product has been tampered with and people are being poisoned, that sure is bad news. Yet conducting interviews out in the open will dramatize your concern and sincerity. Your openness will assist you in beginning the process of rebuilding public confidence in your product and your company.

Yet on other occasions, a development in your organization may warrant turning down an interview. Suppose several members of your team are caught in an illegal activity. You want to get it out and clear the air, but you don't want to subject yourself to a reporter's questions. In this circumstance, rather than agree to interviews, you may just want to release a carefully crafted statement about the matter — saying what you want to say, no more and no less. While still offering a comment, the statement puts some distance between you and the bad news.

This is particularly significant when dealing with television news. If the story is really bad, it may be better to have an "objective" anchorman reciting a quote or two from a "company spokesperson" than for you to appear on camera under duress. At that moment in time, the anchor has more credibility than you do, and his delivery of your explanation of the bad news can actually give it more validity.

Then there are those cases when you know beyond a doubt that a pending story will be negative. Perhaps it is an "investigative" article in which the reporter is out to prove a conclusion he or she has already reached.

You have the option of refusing to be interviewed and instead asking for questions to be submitted in writing as well as the necessary time to research and prepare your replies. You may then submit your answers in writing as well.

As a news maker, you have rights, too! If you don't want to be interviewed, don't do it. If you want to deal with questions in writing, ask for it. If you need time to prepare your response, don't get put on the spot: Demand that time!

Even when the news is bad, I almost always recommend some form of response other than "no comment." You don't have to submit to the third degree on every occasion, but if you refuse to say anything at all in any form, you aren't even in the game.

Now, let's see the results of Cindy's careful preparation. It's four PM. Time for John Acidpen . . . .

The Interview:
Answer Your Own
Questions

"Newspapers always excite curiosity. No one ever lays one down without a feeling of disappointment."

Charles Lamb

How would you like to be both the interviewee and the interviewer? You can be. You should be.

I don't mean literally, of course. Few of us have the gumption to do what Paul McCartney did when he announced the breakup of the Beatles. As you may recall, he did it by interviewing himself and placing a copy of the "transcript" of questions and answers in the jacket of his first solo album. One individual had taken total control over what appeared to be a two-person dialogue.

You may not be able to achieve that level of control, but, to a surprising degree, you *can* direct the course of interviews and shape the content of stories.

John and Cindy Are At It Again!

Let's look in . . . .

Cindy Smoothtalker: Come in, John. Can I get you some coffee or a soft drink?

John Acidpen: No, thanks.

Cindy: I heard you have a new managing editor over there. How are things working out? Has she made any big changes?

John: Jill Johnson. She's been a breath of fresh air. People were nervous at first, but she's instilled a new enthusiasm in the newsroom.

Cindy: You want to talk about the EPA report?

John: Yes. Does your company have any reaction?

Cindy: We certainly do. We're very concerned about it. The health of this community is important to us, too. We breathe the air. We drink the water. So even though the EPA report in no way mentions this facility, our company will conduct an immediate review of our manufacturing and waste disposal process to determine whether compounds used here are the same ones found in the ground water. There will also be a complete inspection of the integrity of our on-site chemical waste-holding areas. Finally, we have communicated with the EPA asking for full and complete access to all lab reports so that we can more quickly determine if part of the problem originates here.

John: But it's pretty obvious, isn't it? Your industrial process uses the same chemical elements that were found in the ground water. The contamination wasn't caused by a handyman incorrectly disposing of a can of paint. It seems pretty clear that your company is responsible.

Cindy: That's an unfair conclusion. These chemicals could come from several sources. That's why we've asked EPA for a full disclosure of the findings so that we can help determine the pollution's cause. When we do, we'll lend our expertise, as concerned members of this community, to solving the problem. And we'll do so whether we're directly responsible or not.

John: Isn't this report one more indication of the Hometown industrial community's real lack of concern for the quality of life?

Cindy: No one can fairly say this when you consider that we provide over five thousand jobs for Hometown residents — and a steady job is pretty important to one's quality of life. We have also sponsored many community activities. We're a responsible corporate citizen in this city, and the record shows that clearly and unmistakably.

John: So you are essentially dismissing EPA's report?

Cindy: I haven't done that at all, John. Can we talk off the record for a minute?

John: Sure.

Cindy: It's widely recognized — in fact you've written on this subject yourself — that EPA has very little credibility when it comes to toxics. I think they're feeling the heat back in Washington, so they're trying to pass the buck. They're looking for scapegoats. That's why we have called upon the agency to provide full documentation of their lab reports, including dates of field tests. Were there new tests that prompted this report? Or is this just a rehash of old data? If so, what prompted the report at this time?

John: One more question?

Cindy: On the record?

John: Yes. If it is determined that your company is responsible, will you pay for the cleanup?

Cindy: We're already paying for toxic cleanup under a formula assessment of industrial companies by the state and federal governments. That's how Congress and the legislature have determined that these things should be paid for, so we'll rely on that system. In addition, if there are any shortcomings in our on-site disposal system, and right now there is no evidence that there are, we will, of course, correct them immediately.

What You Can Learn from John and Cindy

Let's draw some lessons from this exchange:

One: *Cindy was relaxed, confident, and friendly.*

Two: *She broke the ice* by noting a development at John's paper.

Three: *She took charge of the conversation* by deciding when the small talk would end and the inquisition would begin.

Four: *Regardless of what the first question was, Cindy's first answer would have been the same* — a basic statement touching on the major themes the company wants to convey to the public: concern, an effort to humanize the company, and the announcement of affirmative steps. In other words, *Cindy took the offensive.* She gave John a positive news angle to counteract the potentially negative angle he obviously relished: the EPA report.

Five: Once the basic message was out, *she picked apart the report in subtle ways*, but she did not glibly or defensively dismiss it. Nor did she throw blame around or seem uncaring.

Six: *When John was off base, she told him so*, without losing her temper and without getting personal. *She stood up for her company.* She was forthright and cooperative but, again, gave out only as much information as she wanted to.

Seven: In a careful and selective way, *she went off the record* to undermine the credibility of the EPA report and even to give John another possible news lead. But the essential on-the-record message was one of concern and action, not nonchalance or evasion.

Eight: *She clearly established when she was back "on the record."*

What Not to Do in the Interview

Before you assume that Cindy's mastery of this interview was easily achieved, let's look at how the conversation could have gone if Cindy had lost her cool or had not carefully prepared:

Cindy: Come on in, John. What can I do for you?

John: What is your company's reaction to EPA's report that Hometown's ground water is contaminated by toxics?

Cindy: We don't take it seriously at all. These reports are a dime a dozen. It doesn't even mention our company. We don't believe in polluting the environment, but what would you do, close down the whole plant and throw people out of work? That's the kind of damage this environmental movement has caused.

John: You mean you don't intend to do anything about this report?

Cindy: Well, we'll certainly study it, but, again, why should we be asked to do anything? It doesn't even mention our company.

John: But it's pretty clear that your company is responsible because the contaminants found in the water are the same ones used in your production process. Wouldn't you say there's some responsibility on your part?

Cindy: Don't try to put words in my mouth. You called me on short notice for an interview. I gave you an interview. If you want to approach this thing fairly, I'll be glad to talk to you. If not, I have no other comment.

John: You haven't answered my question.

Cindy: No comment.

John: Let's try something else. Does your company plan to take any action at all on the report to determine if it's valid?

Cindy: As I said, it doesn't mention us. We're concerned about toxics, yes, but we pay millions of dollars in taxes to the state and federal governments to find answers and they haven't found any. I'll tell you this, though, your real culprit is not this company but Hometown Steel up river. They could care less about the health of the public.

John: If it is determined that . . .

Cindy: By the way, before we go further, that last comment was off the record.

John: I'm sorry, we were clearly on the record.

Cindy: I'm telling you it was off the record. Now I have nothing more to say, except if you want this relationship to continue you'd better show some good faith. You know that I intended that to be off the record.

Clearly, *Cindy II was not prepared*. She and her colleagues had obviously spent all day congratulating themselves on the fact that their company was not specifically mentioned in the report. Their sole message was, "It's not our problem." They failed to recognize that good press requires more than just a factual presentation but also an emotional one that appeals to the public's concerns. And, it requires a tactical strategy to deal with a suspicious, cynical reporter who is already determined to blame the company.

Cindy I was just as determined to convey the fact that her company was not mentioned in the report; but she did not dismiss the report or say that she didn't care. She recognized that in a public relations sense, it was her problem, simply by virtue of the fact that the press automatically looked to industry as the culprit. While expressing several times the fact that her company was not mentioned, Cindy I still demonstrated concern and action.

Cindy I was cool and professional. She wasn't a patsy. She stood up for her company without being defensive and argumentative. She was forthright, even though she offered only what she wanted to say.

Cindy II was argumentative and even abusive. On one occasion, she refused to comment. She tried to pass blame in a petty, name-calling way and then, realizing she had lost her cool, tried to set retroactive ground rules. She undercut her credibility. She made a sweeping condemnation of the environmental movement, a wholly antagonistic and gratuitous stance.

If John is set on writing a story critical of Hometown's manufacturing concerns, no one interview will turn him around. But even if this story contains a negative premise, there is no question that Cindy I has earned a more favorable portrayal than Cindy II. Her approach will help her in future stories on other topics as well. Because the company was able to respond quickly with some positive steps and because Cindy I was able to express this action and concern, she may have even succeeded in turning a negative story into a positive one.

Interview Guidelines Worth Remembering

Let's review the basic rules, some of which Cindy I remembered and Cindy II forgot:

- Return reporters' calls promptly.
- Don't be afraid to inquire about the subjects to be covered.
- Clearly establish the ground rules before you comment.
- Do your homework on the subject, the reporter, and the news organization.
- Show interest in the reporter's work.
- Show a willingness to be helpful.
- Anticipate questions and prepare answers in advance.

- Devise a central message or theme you want to convey to the public, one that addresses the public's concerns. Reinforce it several times during the interview, particularly at the beginning and the end.

- Don't feel compelled to answer every detail of every question if you don't want to.

- Forcefully present your views, but don't be unnecessarily argumentative and antagonistic.

- Never say "no comment." It has all the appearances of taking the Fifth Amendment. If you don't like a specific question, say something like, "Well, that question neglects the real issue here, which is . . . " and then reiterate your basic theme.

- If you can't answer a question because you don't have the facts at hand, say so, and tell the reporter you'll get the answers later. Don't try to wing it.

- Tell the truth. Honesty really is the best policy — and it's the right policy.

The Real Purpose of the Interview

If you follow these simple guidelines and use them in conjunction with the relationship-building exercises we discussed earlier, your interviews should produce pleasing results. The fundamental lesson is this:

The interview is a question-and-answer session in form only, not substance. Only when you understand that the interview is a communications ritual in which your primary function is not to answer the questions of an employee of a news organization but to convey a message to the public will you be able to dramatically improve your chances for good press.

Never conduct an interview blindly. Know the subject on the reporter's mind and decide up front what your posture will be. Many reporters are well trained in the art of probing. If they don't get an answer they believe is forthcoming (or the answer they want to hear), they will ask the question again and again in different ways.

I'm not suggesting that reporters are "out to get you." They are doing the job as they see it, and that includes probing and challenging your viewpoints.

You are being tested in an interview. Your challenge is to be cool and confident on the outside while always on guard on the inside. From the moment the reporter walks into your office until the moment he walks out, watch what you say. Say only what you have decided you want to say. Make your points forcefully and without hesitation, factually and truthfully, and you will win respect and fairness from most reporters.

Later on, we'll practice some more interview scenarios, but first, let's discuss a very special kind of interview, one where your power of communication is magnified thousands if not a million times over — your appearance on television.

71

Seize the Power of Television

"TV — Chewing Gum for the Eyes"

Frank Lloyd Wright

Let's say that you are invited to make a speech on a complex topic. You ask how long you're supposed to talk. The answer? Twenty seconds.

Could you do it? If you want to communicate effectively on television, you'd better learn.

Television has become the principal medium of news and entertainment for the modern world. In some nations, controlling the airwaves is essential to maintaining political power. The government-controlled television station is often a military coup's first target.

In America, sixty-five percent of those interviewed told a pollster that they rely primarily on television for their news and information. When asked whose version of conflicting news reports they would trust, fifty-three percent of the interviewees favored the television version while twenty-two percent preferred the newspaper report. This apparent faith in television has grown since 1959: At that time, only twenty-nine percent of those polled trusted the television account and thirty-two percent relied on the newspaper's.[1]

The influence of the camera goes far beyond the size of the television audience. Television has changed the way we talk, the way we entertain ourselves, the way we learn, and the way we consume. It has affected the lifestyles of our families and our communities. It has changed politics and the presidency forever and has even directed the course of our foreign policy.

One example which has been much discussed is the case of the fifty-two American hostages held in Iran from 1979-1981. Television's coverage of the crisis personalized the captives in such an intimate way that it effectively narrowed the government's options in dealing with it.

The hostages became next-door neighbors to the American people, who aren't in the habit of allowing neighbors to become sacrificial pawns in international power games. They opposed any action that would result in the hostages' deaths, even if that action might have saved more lives in the future.

The difference between those future victims and the fifty-two hostages is that the latter group and their families had spent dozens of hours in the intimacy of our living rooms. The former group was an abstraction. Television made the difference.

During the same period roughly 100,000 American men, women, and children died in automobile accidents across the country. Many of these accidents were graphically displayed on local news broadcasts, yet television had no way to emotionally capture the magnitude of the story. That's because television is not an expansive medium; it is one that zeroes in on a specific life, detail, or event and brings that cynosure into the confines of our homes.

Some argue that this is good. If television forces our leaders to put people first, all power to it. Others are concerned that television's exposure of human-interest elements actually distorts reality to the detriment of society as a whole. In the Iranian hostage case, they argue, public concern for the foreign service personnel — who knew the profession's risks when they signed on — forced the nation into a policy of abetting terrorism that has since cost many more innocent lives.

Take another example, which you have undoubtedly seen on the evening news:

A network news program opens with a report that the American economy grew solidly in the third quarter. GNP was up at an annual rate of six percent after inflation.

"However," says the anchorman, "as Parker Smith reports, this new economic resurgence has left some communities behind . . . ."

What follows is a film report of unemployed men idling on the street corner. A padlocked factory gate. A tearful woman describing what it's like to lose one's home. The back drop, a gray, drizzly day in this factory town, only heightens the feeling of depression.

Never mind that many more people have progressed economically in recent months; reporters can and do report the percentages. But to the subjective and selective eye of television, the story of this pocket of poverty is more gripping, more compelling, more real.

Television Can Dehumanize, Too!

If television giveth, television can also taketh away. The same detailed scrutiny that can humanize can also terrorize. Television exaggerates every facial flaw or imperfection. Every bead of sweat. Every hair out of place. Every nervous gesture. It can reduce complex issues to simple morality plays between those television chooses to make heroes and those it chooses to make villains, with very few moral shades in between.

During the Watergate scandal, for example, the sweaty, nervous, shifty-eyed Nixon was clearly perceived as "the heavy." This image was reinforced by the retinue of spartan "soldiers" surrounding him, resolutely holding out their bare arms to the flame rather than "ratting" on the kingpin.

The white hats were worn by a handful of senators, none of whom, except perhaps for Senator Sam Ervin, had distinguished himself before in the national media. Ervin had gained notoriety as one of the staunchest defenders of the Southern caste system where being white and male made all the difference. Yet, he, his colleagues, aggressive young prosecutors, and reporters became folk heroes who could do no wrong. Their motives were never in doubt. They weren't concerned about fame and fortune and writing best sellers. Saving the country was their only motive.

Watergate involved terrible wrongdoing. There's no debate about that. Yet, the point is that television oversimplified a complex issue, creating a soap-opera-like drama of right and wrong, good and evil.

77

Thus, paradoxically, although the questions will be fewer and your answers shorter, preparation for a television interview is even *more* compelling than that for a print interview. You must concern yourself not only with what you say and how you say it but also with how you look.

The Preparation

You may notice some significant differences in style between newspaper and television reporters. As discussed earlier, a television station will likely have fewer reporters than a newspaper; consequently, the TV reporter will be less specialized. He or she will focus on the broad outlines of a story rather than pursue every "between the lines" angle.

This could be to your advantage or disadvantage. The TV reporter may not hit you with some of the pointed questioning or argumentative probing that characterize a print journalist's style. He will be more inclined to paint the portrait in broad brush strokes.

TV reporters will also be less likely to have a real conversation with you. Usually, they simply want to film your quick comment and fit it together with several other pieces of film in the editing room. They may ask only several questions. You may have only one or two good shots at an effective answer.

The issue is, will your activities be summarized positively or negatively? Again, preparation is critical. You need to know the same body of facts that you would need for a print interview. But you must craft your responses into catchy quotes for this unique, powerful medium. The subtleties of a long, carefully strategized talk with John Acidpen are out — the artistic creation of a direct, down-to-earth, ten- to twenty-second, ear-grabbing, eye-catching response is in.

In a television interview, the reporter may, in fact, be little more than a prop. At times, he doesn't even appear in the piece, and you have more of an opportunity to say what you want. At the same time, you face stiffer competition, since each story relies on other sights and sounds that may be more compelling to the viewer than your honest face.

And then there's time. Seconds are an eternity in television. Unless you are on a talk show, you will have, at the most, twenty seconds and two or three sentences to get your entire message across. And yet the audience viewing your one comment on TV may be ten times the size of the audience reading your ten quotes in the local newspaper.

Think and Talk in Pictures

Given the importance of your brief television encounter, you should be prepared with your one- and two-sentence responses before you enter the studio.

You should also be imaginative with the use of props and setting. Television loves pictures! When preparing for an interview or appearance, train yourself to think in television images.

Shortly after taking office in 1981, President Ronald Reagan delivered a nationally televised speech on the economy. He wanted to dramatize what had happened to the buying power of the dollar in previous years. Rather than quoting a statistic, he pulled a real dollar out of his pocket and crinkled it before the cameras. Then, as he jingled thirty-six cents in coins in his other hand, he said, "Here is what it's worth today." Quite a potent image!

You can quickly develop similar techniques. Suppose a TV crew is coming over to cover your company's recent decision to hire two hundred more workers. Don't make the announcement or take questions in your chandeliered office. Get your business suit off, your plant smock, hard hat, and protective glasses on, and go to the factory to announce the good news. Make sure workers are hustling and bustling in the background. Attend to small details, such as having the company's name printed boldly across the front of your hat.

Remember that television is primarily a medium of fleeting snapshot images, not of words.

Dressing for the Tube:
An Adviser to Six Presidents
Has Some Tips for You

Your challenge on television is not only to make pictures with your words (we'll discuss how later) but to make a picture frame of your physical appearance.

A picture frame is precisely what your wardrobe should become, according to veteran media consultant Lillian Brown. Brown has applied makeup to the visages of six American presidents as well as business and congressional leaders. She has also consulted with them on wardrobe, voice, and physical movements. I spoke to Brown and asked her what rules are most important to remember in dressing for the camera.

"For both men and women," Brown told me, "I recommend clothes in the middle of the color spectrum. Nothing too light and nothing too dark. You aren't dressing for a garden party and you aren't dressing for a funeral. It's also important not to wear anything shiny, like jewelry or shimmering neckties.

"Please, don't wear white shirts. Gray shirts are the best. The necktie should be plain, either a solid fabric or an understated print.

"My advice for women is similar. Colors in the middle of the spectrum are the best. Please, don't wear gaudy jewelry or bright red lipstick.

"You may have noticed that my dress code for television is rather plain — soft, dark colors; minimal pattern; and monotone outfits. That's because the clothes are supposed to be the picture frame, not the picture itself. I'm not suggesting that you dress cheaply. In fact, I recommend that you buy one expensive wardrobe for TV interviews. Get the best and use it again and again."

Brown also asked me to help dispel a myth. "For some reason," she said, "there is an article of faith going around that men should wear red ties on television to emit boldness and decisiveness. No. No. No. When I watch a man with a red necktie being interviewed,

I watch the tie and not the face. Unless he owns a fashion company and his purpose is to sell ties, I don't think this is where he wants a viewer's eyes directed. A deep maroon is as close to red as I'd recommend in a necktie.

"On television, you want to exude confidence and solidity. Your clothes should be neither flashy nor somber but plain, conservative, and expensive-looking. Needless to say, they should be immaculately pressed and every hair should be in place before going on camera."

Brown offers one more suggestion on preparing your appearance for television. If it is a studio appearance and makeup is available, by all means don't refuse.

Women, you may think that a lifetime of experience applying your own makeup makes you an expert, but not when it comes to the TV camera. Men, don't be shy or bashful. Let them put that makeup on! You'll look great on television and no one outside the studio will ever know.

The television camera is a magnifying glass, revealing every flattering and unflattering feature of your appearance. If you are disheveled, perspiring, or too flashy, you will diminish your credibility and distract the audience from your message.

The Open-Mike Syndrome

One more precaution while you are warming up for the big event: Beware of the open-mike syndrome!

This monster has snared thousands of television performers, reporters, and news makers at one time or another in their careers. Even an experienced performer like Ronald Reagan has made several infamous remarks into microphones he thought were turned off. (Remember "The bombing starts in five minutes"?)

Keep in mind a simple rule. Whenever a microphone is within range of your voice, always, always assume that someone is listening on the other end. That doesn't mean you have to sit there in cold,

81

icy silence before an interview. Just pretend the interview has already started and say nothing you wouldn't say to thousands of people in an "official" interview.

During the Interview

Lillian Brown tells us that how you sit and what body language you use during a TV interview are as important as what you say. Don't slouch back in your chair or hunch forward. Sit up straight with your legs uncrossed; you can't talk properly when your legs are crossed, she says. Better yet, pull your heels back under your chair. This forces you to sit up straight. Keep your hands folded gently in your lap; if you leave them on the desk, your collar will bunch up, giving you that "Hunchback of Notre Dame" look.

Your body language should communicate confidence, alertness, and a keen interest in the person to whom you're talking. Don't scowl or look too serious — even if the topic is serious. Always keep your chin level with the floor (rather than pointing downward) so that the studio lights will highlight your face.

As the reporter directs questions to you, answer the reporter, not the camera. Have a conversation with the interviewer. Occasionally, you may glance to the camera for emphasis, but don't linger too long. It's tantamount to staring at someone directly in the eyes for an extended period of time. We all know how uncomfortable that can be.

Notice that when President Reagan gives a televised speech, he holds a sheath of papers in front of him. Technically, this is unnecessary, because the entire speech is displayed on a glass screen (called a TelePrompTer) directly below the camera. If something goes wrong with the TelePrompTer, the pages come in handy! But they serve primarily as a prop so that the president can break his stare into the camera with a quick downward look. It makes the audience feel more comfortable.

The Comfort Factor

Comfort is what television is all about. We spoke earlier of its power to simplify and generalize. Remember that you are not pounding out your points in a vast auditorium. You have been invited into people's homes. There's no need to shout across the living room. Overactive gestures and voice inflections are jarring and abrasive to television viewers. They will tune you out, turn you down, or turn you off.

It has often been remarked that Senator Edward Kennedy is one of the country's best platform speakers — and that he is. But often when his speech before the faithful is replayed on television, he's awful. That's because he's huffing and puffing, screaming and sweating — and all that passion and energy simply can't fit onto a nineteen-inch screen or in a fifteen-by-eighteen-foot living room.

By contrast, President Reagan is much better on television than he is in a live speech setting. His velvety voice and superb control over small facial muscles are well suited to TV's intimacy. But view him from two hundred feet away and many of his performer's nuances are lost.

This doesn't mean that you should fail to show emotion, passion, or conviction on television. But recall the medium's power to magnify. Communicate through facial expressions and subtle voice modulations instead of excessive hand and body motions.

The camera focuses on your head. Your entire image is encompassed in a screen that is not much larger. Express emotions and sincerity throughout, but do so calmly with a quiet reassurance. Relax your facial muscles and let your warmth, conviction, trustworthiness, and expertise shine through.

Clear your throat and scratch your nose before you go on. Be careful not to drum your fingers on the desk, bounce your leg up and down, or display other nervous habits. And *never* interrupt the reporter or another guest no matter how great the temptation.

All the preparation in the world may not stifle those butterflies when you are in the television studio about to be interviewed. Most of us have spoken before real live people, and we have either conquered stage fright or have learned to keep it in check. But many have not had the opportunity to appear on television, and newcomers to this medium will likely be apprehensive upon entering the strange mechanical world of the studio.

No one has invented a perfect method to eliminate "studio fright," but some experts say you can minimize anxiety by asking questions before going on, like where you should look, where the cameras are, how you should sit, and where you should keep your hands. Don't be afraid to reveal your inexperience by remaining silent.

Then, shortly before the interview, try engaging in some excessive yawning to relax your facial and throat muscles and to get that extra dose of oxygen. Take a small drink of water and try stretching to help you relax.

Be Brief, Be Punchy, Be Quotable

I have watched dozens of experts in their fields proudly sail before the cameras only to submerge their expertise and personality in a sea of confusing sentences, irrelevant examples, and meandering thoughts. Here's a representative sample:

TV Reporter: Mr. Stockwood, should investors be buying stocks or selling them in today's market?

Mr. Stockwood: It all depends on what the Federal Reserve Board does to effect M1, because that has a direct impact on the prime. If the first goes up, the second should come down.

If that's the case, the blue chips are the best bets for buys at this time. If not, you'll see the bears take over on Wall Street and you will see a ratcheting down in the industrials.

This response contains some informed advice and sound reasoning — if you can understand it. Some viewers will, but most will not.

Don't fall into Mr. Stockwood's trap. Instead, offer clear and brief responses to questions. Use personal examples and vivid analogies. Avoid statistics, except for the most general; avoid jargon, except for the most obvious.

Suppose Mr. Stockwood had been appearing on the "Money Matters" section of the local evening news. He would have been better understood by more people if he had said this:

TV Reporter: Mr. Stockwood, should investors be buying stocks or selling them?

Mr. Stockwood: Let me tell you what *I'm* going to do. Tomorrow, the chairman of the Federal Reserve Board, the man who decides how much money will float around the economy for investment and growth, will make an announcement. If he announces steps to increase that supply, confidence in our future is going to blast off like a rocket. I want to be on board, so I'll be shopping for stocks. If you've got the money, you should be, too.

This time, Mr. Stockwood avoided jargon and shop talk. Instead of giving an economics lesson, he offered some personal advice on what average consumers should look for and do. His simply stated, catchy response made an effective television presentation.

With practice, you, too, can become an effective television performer. Be mindful of the medium's power to magnify, simplify, humanize, and distort. Take the positive steps I have outlined and develop a new way of talking when you appear on the tube. In the next Strategy, we'll practice these valued skills.

85

Learn Through Practice and Example

"News is the first rough draft of history."

Ben Bradlee

Effective communication takes some simple preparations and a lot of practice. If you are willing to make the commitment, before you know it, winning them over will become second nature!

Recalling the pointers and preparations from the previous Strategies, let's work on interview skills.

You may notice that in most of the scenarios in *Winning Them Over*, the "bad" example is never so appallingly bad as to make a mockery of the comparison. There may be some good points and nice phrases in the examples I'm asking you to avoid. But our goal is not just to survive but to excel.

I recommend two main practice formats. The first is to work through the interview scenarios in this chapter to see how they manifest the lessons we've been discussing. Then, create some of your own scenarios that parallel your real-life situation. For example, if you run a small company with an innovative product, think about how you would respond to an interview about your business. Don't just toss easy questions at yourself; include some hard ones as well. You may wish to practice with a friend or colleague, particularly as you prepare for a specific interview.

The other practice format emphasizes learning by example. Read newspaper articles and watch television broadcasts in a new way. Instead of focusing on content and information, examine who is being quoted and what they have had to say to be quoted. Critique the performances, appearances, and responses of news makers being interviewed on television. Were they quick, punchy, and quotable or confusing, annoying, and dull?

Scenario One

You are a bank spokesperson invited by a local TV news host to discuss high interest rates and where you think they're headed in the next year.

Interview One

Question: Why are interest rates so high?

Answer: It's important to distinguish between real interest rates and the rates you pay when you make a purchase on credit. Real rates represent the difference between what you pay and the rate of inflation. It's the margin of profit, if you will, for the bank. With the prospect of inflation going up and so many consumers defaulting on loans, that margin is really not that high. By historical standards, they have averaged three percent. Today, they are just about four percent. That extra point is for the extra risk.

Interview Two

Question: Why are interest rates so high?

Answer: Being a consumer myself, I don't like these high rates any more than you do. I think they're going to come down. We all can help pressure them down by shopping around for a favorable rate. If you're in the market for money, call several banks and ask them what their interest rates are. There are some good buys out there if you take the time to look.

Which answer do you like better? If you happen to be a banker or an economic expert, you might think that the first answer was more intellectually sound. But I believe the second is the better reply. Local news programs are interested in passing on to viewers some useful consumer-oriented information, not insights into the complexities of international finance. The second response was less esoteric and more concerned with the average person. The banker got right to the point rather than taking viewers all the way back to World War II.

Scenario Two

You have just been elected president of your PTA at a difficult time — teachers have gone on strike. You sympathize with the teachers, but you oppose a strike. You want to help build pressure for a settlement without taking sides.

Interview One

Question: Do you think that a strike is warranted?

Answer: The parents, teachers, and administrators of this community must make the children their top priority. I don't think the teachers or management should allow the situation to come to this.

I'd like to ask the leaders of both sides, when *they* were kids, how many strikes disrupted *their* schooling? I'll bet you can't find one who suffered through a strike. They don't know what it's like. The parents and children of our town now do, and we don't like it.

Question: How would you resolve this situation?

Answer: First, I think the teachers should return tomorrow, but something else should happen tomorrow as well. The board should convene an all-day session and they should not adjourn until they have settled on a new contract. I'm going to call the leaders of both sides to pursue this good-faith commitment. Parents, if you think this is a good idea, then I urge you to call as well.

Interview Two

Question: Do you think a strike is warranted?

Answer: I think it's irresponsible of them. We'd all like more money, and I suppose they deserve it. I frankly think it's mainly a few leaders who have incited the rest of them. Management has been totally unresponsive as well. I get the idea that everyone would like a vacation.

Question: How would you resolve the situation?

Answer: That's really before management and labor and the collective bargaining process. I really don't want to comment.

The second interviewee's answers were shorter and even punchier, but they were much less diplomatic. If the PTA president's goal is to act like a leader and a conciliator, then the first responses were better. The first respondent pulled all sorts of emotional strings — the concern about the future, the harkening back to a simpler American past. She offered a positive initiative rather than a "no comment." She remembered who her real audience was and she spoke in human terms directly to that audience.

Scenario Three

You're a company executive and you have just announced a new expansion of the plant. You're being interviewed about it on television.

Interview One

Question: There have been reports that your new facility will push our already overtaxed sewage system beyond the breaking point. Do you agree?

Answer: Our analysis shows that the new facility will add only an additional four thousand cubic feet of Level II discharges per month. The dioxides level increase would be virtually nil. The air would be impacted only to the extent that some additional emissions of harmless smoke occur, but our new scrubbers will take care of it.

Interview Two

Question: There have been reports that your new facility will push our already overtaxed sewage system beyond the breaking point. Do you agree?

Answer: This project is the best economic news this town has had in ten years. Two thousand more workers will bring home paychecks to their families. It will benefit the human environment immensely, and we'll do our best to see that it doesn't harm the physical environment.

The second executive refused to allow a somewhat negative reporter to rain on his company's parade. He emphasized the positive. The first executive gave an engineer's response, using abstract terms to contrast risks and benefits.

Scenario Four

The company has just received some bad news. In the third quarter, it not only failed to produce a profit, it posted a loss. You are called by a reporter to explain.

Interview One

Question: How does the company explain this report?

Answer: We're not concerned about it at all. It's just a blip and, as third quarters go, there's nothing really unusual about it.

Question: But this is the first time you've had a drop in a third quarter in almost ten years.

Answer: Well, I don't know where you get your information. I said we're not concerned about it. This company is solid.

Question: Do you think that investors' confidence will be shaken as a result of this decline?

Answer: Only if you folks in the press make a big deal about it. It's just a quarter. These things happen. Your newspaper had a bad third quarter, too.

Now, let's try that interview again, this time remembering the guidelines we have developed:

93

Interview Two

Question: How does the company interpret this report?

Answer: We're not happy about it and we're determined to improve it. We're providing an excellent product for the consumer. That's our primary goal. We also want to provide a good return for our investors. We fell short this quarter, but we'll make it up to them.

Question: Do you think this report will shake the investment community's confidence?

Answer: No, I don't. They know the company is solid. They know that these are difficult times. Our stock fell three points today. I'd say tomorrow is a darn good time to buy!

Ironically, even though the second interviewee more readily acknowledged the obvious bad news, he seemed more upbeat and positive than the first speaker. The second interview was clearly superior. The speaker maintained his credibility and was able to downplay concerns about the company's stability.

Scenario Five

You are a congressman who has been invited to appear on television to discuss your vote for spending cuts.

Interview One

Question: Sir, many people have said that your action shows a disregard for programs designed to keep the poor above the poverty level.

Answer: I voted the way I did because our country is in trouble. We can't go on with these terrible deficits. It will reignite inflation, and that hurts everyone. It will stop economic growth dead in its tracks. I voted the way I did in the best interests of all Americans, especially the disadvantaged who depend the most on solid job growth with low inflation.

Interview Two

Question: Sir, many people have said that your action shows a disregard for programs designed to keep the poor above the poverty level.

Answer: I didn't vote to cut those programs only to reduce the increase they would have normally received. We're still spending more money than ever before on the poor and, frankly, a lot of it's not being well spent. We're maintaining a good, solid commitment to the poor and, at the same time, we're trying to address the deficit problem.

Quick! Which answer is best? This is a tough one, made so deliberately by yours truly. My view is that both responses are potentially good — depending on the congressman's political situation and the kind of audience he wants to reach. Neither response is defensive. Both firmly assert a point of view in short, easily understood sentences. But the first answer is addressed to an audience that perhaps does not care as much about poverty programs as it does about the deficit, the economy, and the creation of jobs. Answer two is designed to reassure a more liberal constituency that the commitment to social welfare is strong. Deficit reduction takes a back seat.

Scenario Six

You have just opened a new bakery in the Hometown shopping mall featuring what you consider to be the best chocolate chip cookie in the world. You are invited to talk about it on the local television's noon program.

95

Interview One

Question: Mrs. Homebake, how are your cookies different from the ones we can buy in the grocery store?

Answer: Well, our cookies are baked fresh every day, without preservatives. We're very proud of our cookies. We think they're the best. I think you will, too.

Interview Two

Question: Mrs. Homebake, how are your cookies different from the ones we can buy in the grocery store?

Answer: Well, I could sit here and tell you how good they are, or I could read you the list of preservatives found in the store-bought cookies which keep them from tasting naturally fresh like mine. But, instead, why not find out for yourself? I brought plenty for my friends here at the station. And, I'd like to invite those of you at home to stop by my shop at Hometown Mall between one and five this afternoon. Tell me you heard about Homebake cookies on Channel Three today, and I'll give you two freshly baked Homebake Chocolate Chip Cookies, absolutely free.

Merely reading these responses, you may have a hard time visualizing this interview. But doesn't the first Mrs. Homebake seem a little nervous and not very imaginative? Giving away cookies may put her small business out of business, but the second Mrs. Homebake took full advantage of a rare, free opportunity to widely advertise her product. She came prepared with a "gimmick" to bring customers to her bakery. As long as her hucksterism doesn't come across as crass, the second Mrs. Homebake is capitalizing on her exposure more dramatically and more successfully than the first.

May I suggest that you continue this practice session during your free moments? You, too, can get your basic points across by communicating in language that people can understand. Use words that go right to the heart of their concerns without going over their heads. Talk in lively, punchy, but diplomatic statements. Be quotable, and you will be quoted!

Generate Free Publicity Seven Ways

"Journalism is the ability to meet the challenge of filling space."

Rebecca West

Strategy Seven stressed the skills you can easily develop to succeed in reporter-initiated interviews. But why wait for reporters to call? After defining their public relations goals, most communicators will find that a major element of their media strategy is to take the offensive and create their own opportunities to tell their story. *You* can initiate many steps to promote your organization and your activities.

I have discussed the importance of developing a network of news media contacts and establishing yourself as a resource reporters frequently call for a quote. But there are other ways to get your message across. Exciting free media opportunities are waiting for you!

The U.S. Chamber of Commerce Model

Dr. Richard Lesher, president of the U.S. Chamber of Commerce, is a man with a mission. In ten years, he has transformed a formerly stodgy, ineffective organization into a dynamic, twenty-first-century communications conglomerate.

The Chamber's work includes lobbying on Capitol Hill, political action, regulatory reform, litigation, international trade policy, and liaison with state and local chambers across the country. But, Lesher says, "The bottom line for the Chamber is communications. We are first and foremost a communications organization."

Upon assuming the Chamber presidency, Lesher quickly realized that the business story would not be told fully and properly until business started doing more of the telling. He turned the Chamber into a communications powerhouse, taking advantage of free media opportunities and creating new ones with the most advanced technology in the business.

Lesher writes a newspaper column called the "Voice of Business" which appears in dozens of publications each week. The Chamber produces a monthly magazine called *Nation's Business* and a weekly syndicated television program called *It's Your Business*.

That's not all. Several years ago, the Chamber embarked on its most exciting and ambitious communications project to date: its own state-of-the-art television studio and satellite communications network called BizNet.

As an individual communicator, you may not have the resources of the U.S. Chamber of Commerce; but you can learn some valuable lessons from its example. Don't wait for someone else to tell your story for you. Tell it yourself. Take the initiative. Win them over!

Seven Valuable Publicity Tools

I. The Press Release

Like the interview, the press release is a key tool of the news profession. You can use it to great advantage in getting your message across. Reporters and editors don't like to admit it but, in many cases, if your release is well written and not overblown, whole chunks of it will appear in a news story as if the reporter wrote it himself. That kind of theft is the ultimate compliment!

Write a press release as you would write a news story, complete with a headline and a lead that captures in one short paragraph the essence of your message. Fill in the details and provide some quotes in the ensuing paragraphs.

Confine your news release to one double-spaced page. If you must run on to a second page, use a second sheet, not the back of the first page.

Clearly identify your organization at the top of the release, but not with a slick, jazzy letterhead. Plain paper or a simple, understated heading has more credibility in newsrooms. Reporters and editors don't like to think they're being driven by a well-oiled public-relations machine. A simple, straightforward heading is better. It connotes that you are communicating some factual information, not peddling your virtues.

You should also note at the top whether the information can be used immediately. If so, type: "Release: IMMEDIATE." If you would like to issue a news release prior to an actual announcement by your organization, include an "embargo" time. Type: "Release: NOT BEFORE 10 AM." News organizations will almost always respect your wishes. Be sure to date all releases. Specify a contact person and phone number in the heading in case a reporter wants to call for additional information.

If you refrain from excessive exaggeration and self- congratulations, the news release — really a "mock" news story — can be a credible and effective way to get your message across.

When you are ready to issue a press release, you can send it through the mail or, depending on time and resources, have it hand-delivered to the appropriate news organizations. I recommend a combination of both methods. Mail the release to magazines, weekly newspapers, and other trade, professional, or news periodicals. But for your major daily paper, key broadcast stations, and local offices of the major wire services (Associated Press and United Press International), I suggest you have the release dropped off in person. This way, you can make sure the newsroom receives the information according to the timetable you have established.

On what occasions or topics should you issue press releases? Organizational announcements, hiring plans, personnel changes, and philanthropic activities all warrant some attention. A release may also be used to convey your reaction to an event.

For example, if you are president of the Board of Realtors and home interest rates have just taken a big drop, you might comment on this development and describe its importance to the housing industry.

Releases can also be used for responding to bad or sensitive news. They give you the opportunity, in the quiet of your office, to carefully develop your response, communicating no more and no less information than you want to.

One habit you should avoid: issuing press releases with no compelling purpose. Just because you woke up in the middle of the night with a brainstorm about a world problem doesn't mean you should publicize it the next day. Your press releases should relate to your area of expertise.

```
OFFICE OF THE GOVERNOR
Sacramento Calif. 95814            RELEASE: Immediate
Kevin Brett, Deputy Press Secretary
Donna Lipper, Assistant Press Secretary        #230
916/445-4571  3-12-86

     Governor George Deukmejian today announced that President

Ronald Reagan and the Federal Emergency Management Agency have

designated Trinity and Nevada Counties for federal disaster

assistance.

     So far, at the request of the Governor, the White House has

approved the following counties for disaster aid:  Alameda,

Alpine, Amador, Butte, Calaveras, Colusa, Conta Costa, Del Norte

El Dorado, Fresno, Glenn, Humbolt, Lake, Lassen, Madera, Marin,

Mendocino, Modoc, Napa, Placer, Plumas, Sacramento, San Joaquin,

San Mateo, Santa Clara, Santa Cruz, Sierra, Solano, Sonoma,

Sutter, Tehama, Tuolumne, Yolo and Yuba.

     Federal Assistance for heavy rains, flood and mudslide

victims could include temporary housing, low interest loans,

individual and family grants, business and farm loans and casualty

loss amendments to previous years tax returns.

     Information about federal disaster assistance can be secured

by contacting the Federal Emergency Management Agency at

415/556-9881.


                          ###
```

The most effective press releases are simple, straightforward presentations of the facts, written in the style of a news story. Although this one does not, press releases can also include a headline and a quotation from the news maker.

If you don't see your choicest press release copy in print every time, relax. While some news organizations may "round file" your releases after one glance, others will read them and file them for future reference — even if they don't immediately act on them. Press releases are an easy, inexpensive way to let the media know you exist.

II. **The News Conference**

Calling a news conference signals that you have a major announcement to make. The following guidelines, offered by executives Voros and Alvarez in their book, *What Happens in Public Relations?*, are invaluable during the preparation stages:

1. A news conference should be reserved for truly major announcements. More than two or three per year, except during a crisis, is probably excessive for a business or corporate sponsor.

2. The most senior management available should conduct the main part of the news conference, but only after thorough familiarization with the subject matter and rehearsal(s).

3. As part of the planning, attention must be paid to every physical detail, such as access to the conference site (particularly if within a large corporate operation), physical and climatic conditions (heating, cooling, light, shelter from elements if outdoors, noise levels, etc.), and fully tested microphones and sound systems, projectors, and other audiovisual aids, complete with trained operators and spare bulbs.

4. Brief but complete announcements for invitations to news media should be sent ten days to two weeks in advance. It is wise to make telephone calls as reminders one or two days before the event. Self-addressed reply postcards are an optional RSVP.

5. Adequate numbers of complete information packages, including full speech texts, captioned photos, and charts, should be on hand for distribution at the beginning of the conference and follow-up distribution later to no-shows.[1]

105

Unless you are a major officeholder, candidate, or celebrity or unless you have just made really dramatic news, stay away from formal news conferences. You can exercise more control when dealing with reporters one-on-one.

I suspect that reporters prefer their own shot at you rather than cover the same event their competitors cover. If you have something on your mind and you want to see it in print, or if you have a beef or a response to a story that has already appeared, don't call an official news conference. Save those opportunities for the times when you have major positive announcements to make.

III. **The News Event**

Also known as a media event, the news event is a carefully staged activity such as an inspection tour, a ground-breaking, or a meeting which has some value for the participants but which is specifically choreographed to be interesting to the news media. Like other media opportunities, such events are often abused, so be careful to maintain your credibility.

Your prime target for news events is television. For example, suppose your medium-size electronics company received a big order for a new, innovative product. You made the announcement to hire more workers, and that was welcome and well-publicized news for your small community. Now, production is underway and the first units are about to roll off the assembly line. Rather than create a standard news release, invite the press to witness the event. Issue a brief, one-page news memo to the relevant media, stating the nature of the event, when and where it will occur, and its significance to the community. Invite their coverage.

Release the news memo several days in advance. Then, the day before, phone the assignment editors or news directors at your television and radio stations. Make a pitch for their coverage. Do the same with your contacts at the newspaper. Remember, you are competing for a scarce commodity — media attention.

Pay particular attention to the visual setting at the factory. Make sure the plant facilities are in order and that the image conveyed is

```
OFFICE OF THE GOVERNOR                    NEWS MEMO
Sacramento, Calif. 95814
Kevin Brett, Deputy Press Secretary
Donna Lipper, Assistant Press Secretary
916-445-4571  3-10-86

     An emergency flood relief measure, providing direct grants

and tax relief to individuals and block grants to counties, will

be signed tomorrow by Governor George Deukmejian.

     The 10:30 a.m. signing ceremony will be held in the President

Ronald Reagan Cabinet Room.

     Your coverage is invited.

                    # # # # # # # #
```

The news memo advises the media in advance of an event which you would like them to cover.

one of contented employees working hard. For the benefit of the cameras, highlight or prominently display the company's name and logo. Keep speeches to a bare minimum. Let the pictures and the happy occasion do the talking!

IV. **Letters to the Editor**

This old stand-by is still one of the easiest and most useful ways to get your message in print, and surveys show the editorial page is a highly read feature in many papers.

Although a letter is often sent in response to a story or to air a complaint, it need not be limited to this. You may wish to echo a point made in an editorial or article or to compliment the paper for its coverage.

Most newspapers publicize guidelines for submitting letters to the editor on the editorial page — guidelines regarding length, format, and where to direct your letter. Keep letters brief and to the point and highly readable. Remember, you're not really talking to the editor but rather to the paper's general readership.

V. **The Op-Ed Article**

One of the great untapped free media opportunities is to write op-ed articles for local, regional, and national newspapers. While these journals are deluged with submissions, they also take seriously their role as a medium for thoughtful opinions expressed by members of the community.

"Op-ed" refers to the page opposite the editorial page, and it is usually the domain of the editorial page editor. In many Sunday papers, this feature is expanded to include a whole section of opinion.

Much of the space on this page is filled by syndicated columnists or regular contributors, but there is room for the ideas of citizens, community leaders, or organization representatives.

The best op-ed piece is not a response to a previous article you didn't like but a creative article which deals with a subject you'd like to raise in a thoughtful and substantial manner. Editorial page editors will not object to your stating a point of view in the piece or even saying good things about your activities or your organization. But they won't look too kindly upon standard boilerplate or company propaganda, either.

George Marotta, public affairs coordinator for the Hoover Institute at Stanford University, describes the op-ed opportunity this way: "These by-lined articles provide an excellent opportunity for the exposure of new ideas or novel analysis of current or future problems facing our society and are usually read by serious-minded persons.

"An op-ed article should concentrate on trying to present only one idea," Marotta advises. "The style of writing should keep in mind the readership of that particular newspaper. A good axiom is to keep it simple and avoid the use of jargon.

"A must for these articles is a good strong lead. The first few paragraphs have to accomplish two objectives: capture the reader's attention and succinctly state the central idea or thesis."[2]

Most newspapers prefer articles that are limited to three double-spaced typewritten pages. That's more than enough space to present a good, well-written, interesting idea. Make sure your submission is free of spelling and grammatical errors and is scrupulously edited. Remember, you are competing with hundreds of others for the precious space on the editorial page.

If you would like to submit an op-ed piece, call the newspaper's editorial office and ask to whom you should direct it. In most cases, you will be dealing with the editorial page editor or a surrogate.

There may be a pleasant side-benefit of this form of communications: Some papers pay a nominal sum for op-ed contributions!

VI. The Radio Actuality

Many communicators overlook the opportunities of radio. You should, of course, send all your news releases and press announcements to the news director of your area radio stations. But that's not all. When you have an important announcement to make or some expert information to offer on a breaking story, you should make available a twenty- to thirty-second recording of your own voice in your own words. This is called a radio actuality.

There are two ways to submit actualities. You can personally call each station and either read your message into its tape recorder or offer a brief telephone interview for later broadcast. But a more efficient process is to record into your own tape recorder and then play the recording over the phone to each station.

For example, if your company is announcing a new hiring, write a concise two- or three-sentence statement. Have a member of your staff play radio announcer by saying into the tape recorder: "Chairman Joe Blow of American Steel today announced the hiring of three thousand workers at the company's Hometown plant. In making the announcement, Chairman Blow had this comment . . . ."

Then record your comment. When you've got it on tape, call the news directors or reporters on duty at the radio stations, and they will tell you whether or not they're interested. Then, using what is called a telephone "coupler," an inexpensive device that fits over the mouthpiece of the phone and plugs into the tape recorder, you can "feed" your statements directly into a radio station tape recorder. Some stations even have a special phone number which, when called, activates an automatic recording device. Listen to the news that evening and you just may hear yourself making news to thousands!

This is an easy method to get some excellent coverage for you and your organization.

VII. **The Broadcast Editorial**

Politicians and commercial advertisers pay thousands of dollars for a precious thirty seconds of air time to promote themselves or their products. You can get sixty seconds of air time, usually before popular early evening game shows, absolutely free.

I am talking about the broadcast editorial.

Most news stations have their general manager or editorial director broadcast opinions on issues of the day on behalf of the station. At the end of these video editorials, they offer "responsible opposing views a reasonable opportunity to reply." That means that if you are sincerely interested in a substantive dialogue (as opposed to mere self-promotion) and if you have the authority to know what you're talking about, you may be selected to write and broadcast an editorial reply.

I remember the editorial director of a major Washington, D.C., television station complaining that she had to practically go begging to find respondents to her editorials; yet she felt a responsibility to inspire such a dialogue. Imagine that! A power center like the nation's capital, and they could barely give away free television time!

If you would like to broadcast an editorial reply, your first step is to call the station's editorial director and let him know. You may not be picked the first time; others may already have volunteered to reply to the same editorial. But keep at it!

If you are selected, follow the station's specifications exactly, to the very second. That's the kind of business television is.

Who should deliver the reply? Gene Fuson, director of KNXT News in Los Angeles, says, "An editorial reply is a sell job. The only difference is you're selling an idea rather than soap, widgets, or deodorants. So use your top salesman.

"The biggest misconception of all is that you must refute, point by point, what the editorial said. The only obligation the replier has is to express a different point of view from that taken by the editorial. That's called free speech."[3]

Construct a simple, clear editorial reply that expresses your theme in easy-to-understand terms. Be direct and forceful. Make sure that whoever goes on camera is fully prepared, rehearsed, and polished.

Opportunity Knocks!

The blessing of our free and diverse media is that they are free and diverse. You don't have to sit around waiting for someone to tell you what's news or forever put yourself at the mercy of reporters. *You* can help decide what's news.

Certainly the interview is an important element in news making. I have emphasized it because getting your message across is toughest when a skeptical reporter filters everything you say. But don't let your media campaign stop with an effort to perform well in front of reporters. As I've demonstrated in this chapter, there are many opportunities to make your case without them. Use these opportunities responsibly, but by all means use them!

Fight Bad Press When It Makes Good Sense

"Always remember that others may hate you, but they won't win unless you hate them back. And then, you destroy yourself."

Richard M. Nixon

In the eight Strategies discussed so far, I have stressed the positive: Simply follow some basic rules and prepare, and you are well on your way to good press.

But things can and do go wrong, particularly when the airing of your message is dependent upon a profession of unpredictable human beings called reporters.

I've urged you to accept some facts of life about your dealings with reporters. You are likely to have an adversarial relationship with many, and you may frequently find yourself dissatisfied with their coverage. I've encouraged you not to let your dissatisfaction deter you from dealing with the press in a positive manner.

Having said that, I also recognize that bad press, unfair press, does occur — a lot! Communicators need a strategy to deal with it.

Let Strategy, Not Emotions, Be Your Guide!

Fighting back feels so good! But so does good press! The two are not always compatible.

Approach bad press, and any decision about whether to fight back, pragmatically — not emotionally. In other words, fight back when it is the best strategy for future good press. Resist when it is not, even if an injustice has been done. Your decision should be based on the seriousness of the transgression and the importance for the future of maintaining a particular press relationship.

Is This Fight Really Necessary?

If you are less than satisfied with a particular news story, step number one is to honestly assess the problem. Was it a grievous injustice, a factual error, or a matter of a few words that rubbed the wrong way?

I know it is hard to separate yourself from your convictions about your organization. But try stepping back from the report in question and asking yourself: Is it really bad, or is it just a case in which the writer didn't reflect our company's preferred self-image? You may decide that the public's view of the article will be generally favorable or at least indifferent — that a battle over a few words or a single uncharitable characterization is just not worth the fight.

Is a Fight Wise?

If you have determined that an error or unfair assessment is of sufficient import to take some action, then you must contemplate the risks. How important is your relationship with the particular reporter and news outlet, and would it be jeopardized by taking action? Do they cover you on a regular basis? Do you need their continued coverage? Is this reporter going to be around and writing about you in the forseeable future? These are critical factors to consider in determining your response to a single story.

If you believe the reporter *is* important to your future communications strategy, you don't have to cower; but you may consider more closely the kind of protest you will make.

After you have evaluated the severity of the crime and the significance of your relationship with the offender, you can choose from a number of actions. Before taking any, though, recognize that your opponent has barrels of ink and complete control over what is printed. You can count on editors to almost instinctively back up their reporters, even when they know in their heart that an error has been committed.

Overkill Can Kill Your Press Coverage

Cross the bridges to open warfare with the press one at a time, because it serves no one to reach that final destination!

- If you feel an error or injustice has occurred in a story, call the reporter and discuss it. If it is a small error, request no specific remedy, just let him know you are watching! This can be done in a friendly, positive manner, particularly if you have developed a good working relationship with the reporter, as advocated in Strategy Three.

- If you feel the mistake or unfair characterization is serious, write a letter to the editor. As a courtesy, tell the reporter you plan to do this.

- Got a beef that requires tougher steps? You should then not only complain to the reporter and the editor but also formally request that a correction or clarification be made in a follow-up story. You could also relate your grievance to the newspaper's ombudsman, whose job it is to discuss in print his own paper's practices and mistakes.

- The next bridge to cross is to go public with your complaint. Write a letter to the editor for publication and issue a statement singling out the news outlet in question or even consider buying space in the paper to reply.

- The final mile to Armageddon is the lawsuit. This is the serious stuff that should be pursued only 1) if all other avenues have been exhausted and 2) if the injustice is so extreme as to warrant an application of our libel laws.

The Squeaky Wheel Gets the Grease

Well, sometimes. Other times, it goes flat! Plan your response to bad press with great care and caution. Make sure a rebuttal is worth the effort and that the punishment fits the crime. In most cases, a simple call to the reporter, friendly and professional, will suffice.

Remember that your goal is to make a favorable impression with the public. Impression. That doesn't mean every story has to confirm every personal quality or organizational attribute. Don't go to war over an inappropriate adjective in paragraph twenty on page thirty-four.

But stand up for your right to fairness! When you think you've been treated badly, you can usually get a hearing and maybe even a retraction. Make yourself heard in a firm, professional manner, but only when you have honestly assessed that the facts are on your side. Above all, let them know you are watching.

Some journalists may be highly critical of my suggestion to write letters to and phone editors. They may call this "intimidation" of the press. I'm not advocating that you become a chronic complainer about your press coverage or that you use your possibly influential position in the community to take unfair advantage of a reporter trying to do his job.

But you've got a job to do, too, and you have a right to expect fair treatment from the media. Like members of any other profession, journalists have to be able to take the heat, too. Fueled by the wrong motives, of course, protest strategies can be abused. But potential for abuse is not sufficient cause for the press to blanketly deny a news maker's right to appeal.

I believe in talking back to the press — when it is justified, when it will help your cause, and when it is done sincerely and professionally.

Win Them Over!

"Put it before them briefly so they will read it, clearly so they will appreciate it, picturesquely so they will remember it, and, above all, accurately so they will be guided by its light."

Joseph Pulitzer

Some of my friends in the media reacted curiously when I questioned them about the styles and secrets of their profession. They indicated that the less we communicators know about the reporting business, the more "honest" we will have to be. To some, divulging news-gathering strategies to news makers is like sharing law enforcement techniques with criminals!

If the media fear that we intend to more effectively communicate with the public through them, that fear is well-founded. That's our mission. That's our right.

Let's review the strategies we will need to effectively tell our stories through the news media.

Strategy One: Make Peace with the Press

News media professionals bring to their work a lifetime of habits, opinions, and biases. Yet the majority try to conduct themselves with integrity. You can expect an adversarial relationship with reporters and, most likely, a number of disputes and contentious moments. Accept the fact that these conditions come with the territory.

Yet also recognize that you need reporters and they need you. They hold important keys to your aspirations to communicate and lead. Develop a strategy to earn your share of fair media attention. Don't allow fear and suspicion to poison the great possibilities for publicity that are waiting for you.

121

Strategy Two: Get Out of Your Bunker

Don't fall into the trap that has snared many executives. Get out of your bunker and chart a positive, aggressive media strategy for generating publicity and news coverage and turning potentially troublesome inquiries into favorable portrayals.

Understand that reporters don't work for you and their stories won't exactly mirror your self-image. Direct your efforts toward producing a greater quantity of positive coverage than negative — with or without the aid of reporters.

Strategy Three: Make Reporters Call on You

If you want to be an effective media communicator, you must develop strong, professional relationships with those whom you expect to carry your message. Methodically conduct a media survey of the important news organizations in your area and your field. Learn about the key media gatekeepers in each newsroom or editorial office. Make introductory phone calls and visits. Develop professional relationships with these gatekeepers and establish yourself as an important resource for them.

In order to increase the quality and quantity of your press coverage, you have to let reporters know you exist. Take positive steps to make this happen.

Strategy Four: Before the Interview: Plan Your Answers

The primary news-gathering ritual is the interview. But your goals in the interview are very different from those of the reporter. His goal is to ask you questions and record your answers. Your goal is to convey exactly the message you want to communicate to the general public.

Prepare diligently for the exchange. Review the reporter's previous work. Anticipate his questions and plan your responses in advance.

Always view the interview as an opportunity, not an ordeal. Enter this intriguing verbal contest positively, confidently, and well prepared.

Strategy Five: The Interview: Answer Your Own Questions

Approach the interview with confidence and firmness. Stick up for what you believe, but don't become argumentative or abusive. Clearly establish the ground rules for your comments, such as whether you are talking "on the record" or "off the record."

Regardless of the specific questions, make sure to emphasize and re-emphasize the basic themes you want to communicate to the public. Remember that your true audience is not the reporter but the reporter's readers, listeners, or viewers.

Always tell the truth, but try to tell it in short, punchy quotes.

Strategy Six: Seize the Power of Television

The power of television to communicate messages to millions is an opportunity no communicator can afford to miss. To perform effectively on television you must:

1. frame your entire message in several sentences which are visual, direct, and catchy. These should be planned and written before you enter the studio;

2. frame your physical appearance with subdued yet elegant clothing and good grooming;

3. respect the intimacy of the medium. Sit up straight and keep your chin level. Do your throat-clearing before you go on camera. Refrain from nervous movements and gestures. Relax your facial muscles, smile, and express emotions and convictions calmly.

Strategy Seven: Learn Through Practice and Example

It takes practice to learn how to talk in quotes, but that's precisely your goal — to speak those memorable phrases and lines which are most likely to make it into print. Practice with the scenarios presented in Strategy Seven and by using your powers of observation and imitation. Look closely at who gets quoted and why.

When preparing for an upcoming interview or television appearance, take the time to write out a scenario reflecting how you think the exchange will proceed. Anticipate the questions and prepare catchy responses. Write them down. You may not recall every word, but if your key phrases are memorable you will remember them — and so will your audience!

Strategy Eight: Generate Free Publicity Seven Ways

You aren't always dependent on reporters when you want to communicate through the news media. There are other outstanding opportunities for media exposure:

1) The press release
2) The news conference
3) The news event
4) Letters to the Editor
5) The op-ed article
6) The radio actuality
7) The broadcast editorial reply

An effective communications strategy must take advantage of these free media opportunities. Reporters can't be expected to do all your work! Tell your story the way *you* want it told!

Strategy Nine: Fight Bad Press When It Makes Good Sense

Bad press comes with the territory. Any decision to fight back must be made strategically, not emotionally. Base your judgment on the seriousness of the transgression as well as on the importance of a continued relationship with the reporter and organization in question.

If you decide to protest, proceed conservatively. Begin with a call to the reporter. Maybe the problem can be worked out between you. If not, assuming the situation is serious enough, contact the editor and ask for a correction or a follow-up story. A lawsuit, or even publicly criticizing the story in a statement or paid advertisement, should be reserved for the most extreme violations.

Strategy Ten: Win Them Over!

You've grown up with the media, from the *Weekly Reader* to your professional journals. How many newspapers have you read in your lifetime? How many radio broadcasts or TV programs have you listened to or watched?

You are the product of a multi-media age. You have more experience and knowledge about media communications than you might imagine. Combine this raw experience, your abilities to observe and persuade, and the simple strategies of this book to turn the news media into a medium for you and your organization.

You won't meet with one-hundred-percent satisfaction every time, and, in our democracy, isn't that healthy? But you can tap the public domain of the press and airwaves to communicate honestly and effectively with your fellow citizens.

There's no other choice. The days of communicating across the garden fence are over.

You have the potential of reaching more people with greater frequency, intensity, and intimacy than ever before in mankind's history. You have the power to touch others with your deepest convictions and most passionate beliefs. Leadership in almost every field depends on your media skills and the extent to which you get your story told. Take the steps in this book and you can transform your dealings with the media from a fearful burden to a golden opportunity. Use your new-found abilities wisely, responsibly, effectively, and win them over!

Another grand opportunity awaits you as a communicator and a leader: the exhilarating high and bankable commodity that come from writing and delivering a blockbuster speech. We've met the challenges of dealing with the news media. In Part Two of *Winning Them Over*, we'll climb that other mountain — and we'll make it to the top there, too!

PART TWO

GIVING POWERFUL SPEECHES: TEN STEPS

Speak with a Strategy

"Mend your speech a little, lest it may mar your fortunes."

Lear, in Shakespeare's *King Lear*

The gentleman must go nameless. A powerful, successful, self-confident man with a lifetime of achievement in industry, he was about to make the principal address at an international business conference.

Several hours before his speech, he decided he didn't like the draft that had been prepared for him. He asked me to rewrite it. "There's no time," I said. "Just see what you can do and bring it up to me during the luncheon," he replied.

I typed furiously. I finished during dessert, minutes before he was scheduled to disclose his economic philosophy and political agenda to the gathered crowd. Feeling conspicuous, I carried the text up to the dais and slipped it to him. He put on his glasses and began to look it over. Just as he started, the emcee's spoon hit the glass, signaling the need for quiet. The speaker was introduced. The nightmare had reached its final chapter.

I'll give you three guesses as to how the speech turned out, and the first two don't count! This witty, intelligent leader, armed with a lifetime of experiences and achievements, blew it. And I was a partner in his crime!

With my help, he broke every speechmaking rule I would like to share with you. It will be useful to remember this outrageous episode not only as you follow the steps I am outlining but also as you break your back in preparation and wonder, "Why the #%&!*#! am I doing this?"

Why Make Speeches?

Most speakers approach their chore with varying degrees of nervousness, fear, and dread. I trust that after you complete the ten steps to giving powerful speeches you will not be one of these. Public speaking is, and should be for you, a gratifying, even exhilarating, activity. For a few special minutes, you are in the spotlight with a grand opportunity to make a vital contribution to your company, career, and community.

We spend most of our lives talking — to family, friends, co-workers, and even strangers across the supermarket check-out counter. Most of our conversations are unpretentious, unrehearsed efforts to convey thoughts, emotions, and instructions and to conduct the daily business of life.

A speech is all that and much more. It's more than an information exchange among relatively equal parties: It's the elevation of one individual to a leadership position. He or she is separated from the others, often physically elevated on a platform. For a significant part of the presentation, conversation is out of form.

A speech embodies in the speaker the potential for near-perfect control over a group's thoughts and actions for a specified period of time. Thus, when you are given the chance to speak, you are receiving an opportunity to lead through the power of words. You have the potential to impress, persuade, sell, entertain, and thus advance your career and better serve your organization. Make the most of the opportunity whenever you are called upon to speak publicly.

In today's complex, fast-paced society, do you sometimes feel that you're losing control — of your career, your surroundings, or your relationships with people? Do you get the feeling that the individual and his or her skills don't matter that much any more?

Dr. Robinson's cure: a speech a day! All the world's a stage and you're on it. All eyes are trained on you. All ears are receptive to your words. The art of speechmaking is surely changing, but it has hardly died. What a fantastic opportunity, an exhilarating high — *if* you take advantage of it.

Move Over, Jane Fonda!

Making a good speech requires a one-hundred-percent "workout" from your body and your heart as well as your brain. But before proceeding to the first workout step, let's consider a compelling question: What is your goal?

- You want to sound good and look good.

- You want them to agree with what you say or at least respect you for saying it.

- You want them to do what you ask them to do.

- You want to win them over.

Later on, I'll discuss those rare cases in which you may actually want to shock and outrage your audience, where your first goal is to get booed. (I'm going to keep you in suspense for awhile as to whether you think I'm crazy!)

But first things first: *Your goal is to impress the audience*. To do that you must do more than compose a good message. If you want to be judged solely on content, why not just submit a written essay and cancel the speech?

What you say is important, of course, but so are a few other factors, like how you sound and how you look; what kind of clothes you're wearing on the outside and what kind of mood you're wearing on the inside; whether you are under-prepared or over-nerved; whether you are funny and eloquent, relaxed and in command; and how you react to the unexpected.

Ignore some or all of these factors and you could be delivering the Gettysburg Address and still fall flat on your face. Acknowledge these variables, take charge of every facet of your appearance and presentation, and you can make the audience fall for you in less than twenty minutes.

Seize the Opportunity!
(But Obey the Rules)

The best kind of speech can be thought of as a *conversation with a strategy*. Conversation — because audiences, while looking up to you as the platform authority, also want to feel that you are accessible to them. Arrogant, bombastic, and overbearing oratory is unsuited for today's audiences.

By the same token, the audience expects more from you than an informal "shoot the bull" session. While maintaining a friendly, conversational manner, you must also carefully structure your arguments, thoughts, and even jokes and make them lead to an overriding persuasive purpose. In other words, empower your conversation by giving it a strategy.

When the president of the United States walks in front of the camera and stands before an audience, it seems like he can say just about anything he wants. Your purpose for speaking, however, is clearly defined by others. As stimulating as speechmaking can be, remember that you're not necessarily on center stage because you're a famous public figure; you're making that speech because you've been given an assignment or because you've been asked to share some specific information. Your first obligation is to do your duty.

Perhaps you have just been elected chairman of your local marketing executive association. Your job is to discuss upcoming plans, activities, and trends in industry in your area, not to share your vision of the twenty-first century.

Maybe you are testifying before a legislative committee, communicating your company's support of a particular bill. The legislators aren't really interested in your theories about the free enterprise system.

Suppose you have been asked to make a presentation to the corporate brass on the activities of your division. Do you really want to share with the chairman of the board your musings about life and love? The audience has invited you (or commanded you) to appear and share your expertise on a particular topic. In most cases, your purpose is right there in plain English — in a memo or an invitation letter, in a program, or in a phone call from the sponsor.

Remember why you are there and why you are not there. Be attentive to your audience and respectful of the forum. Live up to expectations first. Then concern yourself with exceeding those expectations.

This is an especially important lesson for the new speaker. You head into the experience wanting to dazzle the audience with your wit, charm, and personality. You may not be able to do that at first, even after reading this book! Any worthwhile skill takes practice to develop. But let it at least be said of your early efforts that you did a professional and competent job. In this era of bad speeches and worse speakers, competency alone will go a long way toward impressing an audience.

Let's go back to the president for a moment. I began by saying that he can talk about almost anything he wants to. That's not quite true. Even the president is confined by expectations and limited to acceptable dialogue and well-established rituals of government and politics.

If the president invites a group of small business leaders to the White House and then talks about foreign policy, he's breaking the rules. He'll be vigorously applauded, but eyebrows will be raised and opportunities missed. If he goes before a joint session of Congress to talk about the farm crisis and talks instead about the Soviet Union, the Speaker of the House is going to be very, very angry.

When you are asked to speak, you are limited by your assignment and by expectations. Don't pull a fast one on the audience. Since they have to sit and listen to you, they should have some say over the use of their time.

I remember one speaker who chose to bend the rules. He was a participant on a panel of international trade experts at a conference that was attended by the governor of California and other top state officials. Rather than stick to his own agreed-upon topic, he began his presentation by saying, "Before getting into my subject, I would like to offer some observations about the presentation of the previous speaker. I understand that this will come out of the time I have been allotted."

Frowns quickly formed on many faces throughout the audience. To make matters worse, he didn't adhere to his time limit. He tried to give two speeches in a time slot meant for one. As the clock ticked away, he talked faster and more furiously to cover his topic. The frowns turned into outright resentment.

Ironically, this speaker had the most expertise of any guest that afternoon, but this was all lost as he sacrificed his good will with the audience. He failed because he failed to do his job.

If you want freedom of speechmaking, completely removed from social and professional contexts, I have a suggestion to make. Put on a shabby overcoat, buy a bottle of Thunderbird, and don't take it out of the bag. Stand on a street corner and talk about anything you like!

Total freedom in a speech is a speech without a strategy, and that is powerless.

Although Part Two focuses primarily on the speech format, the suggestions are also useful for variations of public speaking such as:

- making formal presentations to peers or superiors in your organization,

- lecturing to a class or symposium,

- leading a panel discussion or participating in a professional conference.

By following the steps outlined, and with sufficient practice, you can confidently approach public speaking, demonstrating the leadership qualities that are in such great demand in almost every field.

Spy on the Audience and Setting

"You may use different sorts of sentences and illustrations before different sorts of audiences, but don't talk down to any audience."

Norman Thomas

I hope you're excited about public speaking. You might respond by saying, "Fearful, yes. Excited — are you crazy?"

Stage fright is as natural as it is inscrutable, and we'll discuss it further in Step Eight. But conceiving of a speech as potentially invigorating is an essential emotional framework. Start thinking of your speech as a unique leadership opportunity rather than an ordeal, and you will soon put your fear in check.

Ready for Step Two? Like most public-speaking guidebooks, mine emphasizes the critical importance of advance preparation. This theme runs through Part One of this book as well. Preparation is essential. You can't execute a successful strategy in a speech if you haven't taken the time to determine exactly what to say and how to say it.

At the same time, most professional men and women are extremely busy. You can't drop everything for a week just because you have to give a twenty-minute speech. Learning some preparations that are not too difficult or time-consuming will help. If you can't follow these guidelines precisely, don't worry, you're not doomed to failure. Speech preparations, like study habits in school, can vary from individual to individual. The task can still get done.

Know Your Territory Blindfolded

To put yourself in a position of authority on that platform, you have to truly be an authority. Learn your topic cold. Make sure you are familiar with every concept and idea introduced in your speech.

Every fact and statistic should stand up to scrutiny. If a question-and-answer period follows, anticipate potential angles of questioning and make sure you are conversant in them.

I once attended a meeting where a division director made an excellent presentation to the chief executive. The subject was job training proposals to help address the unemployment problem in the community. Armed with visual aids, he outlined his proposals in a highly articulate and organized fashion. Yet when he finished, the chairman asked him to review the extent of the unemployment problem in the area and describe how many people the company was currently training. Basic questions, and yet he could not answer them off the top of his head. His confidence crumbled, and we all shared his embarrassment.

In most cases, particularly in speeches you deliver outside your organization, your topical research needs will be relatively uncomplicated. Exhaustive research — in the dusty file cabinet and library sense — is usually not required, assuming you are already an expert in the field you have been called upon to address.

The greater challenge, to be discussed in Step Five, is not to acquire more technical expertise, but to translate the expertise you already have into plain English for a general audience.

Learn to "Spy" on Your Audience

Instead of spending your research time in the library, spend it learning as much as you can about the audience you will be addressing and the environment in which you will be speaking. What you say and how you say it should be determined in large part by to whom you are saying it and where.

Many of us spend a lot of time looking in the mirror. Go on, admit it! But in speech communications, how we look to others is as important as how we look to ourselves. Daily life is a performance for a go-getter, and success requires winning Oscars every day.

Perhaps the best way to understand how crucial is a complete knowledge of the audience and the setting is to consider the great lengths to which major politicians go to prepare for a public appearance.

Before appearing on stage, they usually receive detailed background information from a team of researchers and advance men. Names of head table guests are provided. Diagrams of the auditorium and backstage areas are studied. The route for entering and leaving the hall is pre-determined. Stage arrangements, including the height of the podium and presence of flags and other symbolic or decorative objects, are checked and double-checked.

Format is hammered out in advance. Will questions be allowed after the speech? Is the event open to the news media? What are the audience's special concerns, problems, interests, and complaints?

Why such extraordinary preparations? So the speaker can enter the room confidently, relaxed, and self-assured. Familiar with the audience and the setting, he or she assumes full control of the occasion and can focus complete attention on a powerful speech. The less the speaker has to worry about tripping over an unknown set of stairs, the more attention he can give to the presentation.

Most likely you won't have the luxury of speechwriters, researchers, and advance men. But there are some steps you can take on your own. Before preparing what you're going to say, learn as much as you can about where you're going to say it and to whom you will be speaking.

If this sounds like low-priority detail work, consider some real-life nightmares of those who used to think so:

Nightmare: You're nervous about your speech. You've got the shakes. All you had time to do was scribble out your speech on both sides of crumpled sheets of a yellow legal pad. But once you settle in behind that big, sturdy lectern, you should be all right.

You're introduced and you walk into the room. Nice applause. You turn and head toward the lectern — -except there is no lectern! Just a lonely, thin, solitary stand-up microphone. Anxiety turns into pure terror. You and the audience spend an uncomfortable thirty minutes as you nervously shuffle pages, straining to read your own terrible handwriting. They feel too sorry for you to really hear your message.

141

Solution: A simple phone call to the event organizer determining the availability of a lectern.

Nightmare: You're invited to speak at a company's annual retreat. It takes place in a resort setting and is billed as an informal, relaxing, "let your hair down" three days of BS sessions interspersed with golf and tennis. You're welcomed to bring your tennis shorts and maybe play a set yourself.

You show up to address the morning session. The sun is bright. You arrive early enough to see businessmen and women scurrying back to their rooms, clad in shorts and bathing suits. No problem there, you're in jeans and polo shirt. At the appointed time, you stride confidently into the conference room and gaze out, in shock, at your audience: grim-faced "retreaters" clad in business suits.

Remember the adage about relaxing by picturing the audience naked? How about making a speech in which the audience is looking at you as if *you* were naked! That's what this gentleman felt like.

Solution: A simple phone call to determine the company's precise definition of "let your hair down" and the specific dress code for your part of the program.

Nightmare: You're a school superintendent and you've been invited to speak at an educational symposium, "Education in the 1990s," a three-day event to be attended by other education experts, teachers, students, press, and government officials. You work your heart out on an enthusiastic speech outlining some of the problems facing public schools, the challenges of being a superintendent, and your vision of where public education should be headed.

You arrive at the appointed hour and on the way in you pick up a conference program. You look for your name. It can't be! You're scheduled to lead a detailed discussion in an audience of fellow superintendents about the ways schools can better prepare seniors for higher education! Totally unprepared for that specialized topic, you are faced with some grim choices: deliver an irrelevant speech to a group who knows almost everything you know, or just wing it!

Solution: A simple phone call to pin down your specific role in the conference.

Now, if you have been reading these actual episodes and saying to yourself, how can people be so dumb — believe me, even smart people make these mistakes all the time.

Here is how you can prevent them:

- Once you have agreed to speak, take a few minutes to talk to the organizer. Find out exactly to whom you will be talking. What kind of program has been planned? Who will be speaking before you and after you? How much time has been allotted for your presentation? Does the event have any special themes or purpose? Who will introduce you and how? Will there be a question-and-answer period?

- Next, turn your attention to the setting. Will it be informal and relaxed? Will people be seated theater style or in a circle? Will they be in the middle of coffee and donuts when you get up to speak? Will there be a public address system? A podium and/or a lectern?

You should never hesitate to ask these questions or even to make requests for certain arrangements, such as a lamp on the lectern. The more you know about the environment in which you will be placed and about the audience and the setting, the more appropriate and appealing you can make your presentation. The more you can relax by putting the mundane considerations out of mind, the better you will be able to communicate.

- Whenever possible, visit the site of the speech beforehand. Politicians do this before their major appearances. They walk the route up to the lectern. They get a feel for the stage. They gaze out at where the audience will be. They check to see if the microphone is too high or the lectern too low. Preparations like these prevent surprises and mistakes, the most common of which is that the speechmaker can't see his printed text because a short lectern puts it at a distance further away than he's used to reading without his glasses.

We all have a natural fear of the unknown. By getting as much information ahead of time, you can relax and assume greater control of the opportunities at hand. Here is a simple checklist to help you demystify the speech experience:

1. What topic, be it specific or general, has been assigned to me?

2. How much time has been allotted for my appearance?

3. Who are my hosts? Should they be recognized or thanked in my speech?

4. What is the purpose of the event at which I will be speaking?

5. When should I arrive, when will I begin my speech, and when will it be appropriate for me to leave?

6. How is the program structured? Who else will be speaking before and after me?

7. What type of audience will I be addressing? (professionals, experts, newcomers to the topic, spouses?)

8. How will the audience be seated — theater style, at round tables, in a circle? Will the audience be seated? (Audiences are left standing at many cocktail reception speeches!)

9. Where will I be seated in relation to the lectern?

10. Will a lectern and public address system be provided? What style?

11. Who will introduce me? Can I provide my own biographical information?

12. Will there be news media in attendance, any special guests or individuals I should know about (such as my own boss at the firm!)?

13. Will there be a question-and-answer period after my speech? If so, for how long?

This intelligence can usually be gathered after one or two phone calls to the program sponsors. And even though most of us don't have the time to do this, visiting the scene ahead of time can provide an extra-added bonus of preparation.

The biggest threat to your success in a given speech is the unknown. Take a few minutes, follow as much of the checklist as you can, and slay this dragon!

Selecting and Sizing Up Your Audience

In the beginning of this book, I spoke of the need to identify the specific "publics" you want to reach with your speech and media messages. Understanding the background and make-up of your audience, its likes and dislikes, is critical to effective communicating. Only by understanding the kind of selling job you have to do can you adopt the proper strategy for making the sale.

Does this mean you should change your tune to fit the audience? You bet! Does it mean you should discard principle and say whatever it takes to win applause? Of course not.

Let me draw the distinction. When discussing my role as a speechwriter, I often point out that if I were assigned to write a speech for President Reagan and Governor George Deukmejian on the same topic before the same audience, I would still submit two entirely different speeches — even if their views on the topic were identical.

That's because the two speakers are different. They have different styles and different personalities. When writing a speech for someone else to deliver, I try to capture his unique mannerisms and voice patterns.

If you are speaking on the same topic to two different audiences, respect *their* individual characteristics as well. What persuades one audience may not persuade another. What one group

145

understands may sail right over the heads of another. Be prepared to adopt a different strategy for each audience, and sometimes say things in different ways in order to win them over.

For example:

You are a governor who has had to veto a great deal of spending passed by the legislature in order to get the state out of debt and balance the budget. Your goal before a supportive group is to identify with its philosophy and generate enthusiasm for your policies.

You say: "Our days of debt and deficits are over. While providing amply for the less fortunate, we're doing something quite unusual for government these days. We have balanced the budget — not by raising your taxes but by vetoing billions of dollars in spending instead. We're back in the black and that's where we intend to stay."

But to a skeptical audience you might say this: "Without fiscal health, without a balanced budget, all our basic programs for the sick, poor, and elderly would be threatened. Balancing the budget, even if it requires some vetoes, is a compassionate act for those who truly depend on government."

In both cases, the goal is the same — to justify and promote the desirability of vetoes. The message is the same, but the packaging is different, depending on the audience. The goal of the second speech is to convince a skeptical audience of the desirability of spending reductions. Simply stating that the vetoes have held down tax increases ignores their concerns — in this case, social programs for the disadvantaged. This group needs a waltz. The first group wants a military march!

With practice, you, too, can fine-tune your communications strategy to harmonize with a specific audience. In addition, knowledge about an audience is useful in order to add personalized references about them in your speech. This gives the group the

146

impression that you really care and that you are speaking with conviction directly to them and to no one else.

You should always open your remarks by recognizing by name the individual who introduced you. Say a few nice words about the organization responsible for the event. "Tip your hat" to the president or any other special people in the group. Cite several examples of the fine work being accomplished by the organization.

Again, a word of caution: This is not an invitation to discard principle. Stick up for what you believe. Find compelling, interesting, and unique ways to present your principles. Use your energy and creativity not to run from your positions but to convince a doubting audience to see your way of thinking. At the very least, use your persuasive skills to get them to begin re-examining their assumptions.

The Tough Sell

Audience research is particularly important when that audience will be tough to convince or even downright hostile. If you know that an audience may be resistant to your pitch or oppose your views, you can devise a number of strategies:

Disarm them with sincerity. Establish your credibility by prefacing your remarks with statements such as, "I'm not suggesting this is the only course to take. I'm not suggesting that I have all the answers, but allow me to add to your range of options."

Disarm them with frankness. Deal directly with what you have learned about an audience's doubts. For example, if you are making a proposal to a company executive, you might say: "I know you are considering other options. I know you have concerns about my proposal. I'm here to tell you point by point why this proposal is the best."

Disarm them with subtleties. On other occasions, a subtle approach is more appropriate. You still confront what you have learned to be the audience's reservations, but you do so indirectly.

147

For example, if you represent a small computer company trying to compete with IBM for a potential contract, you will likely learn that the potential client's chief concern is whether or not you can offer the same level of services and repairs.

You could deal with the issue head on, but depending on the audience, you might appear nervous and defensive. Another option is to speak to those concerns without overtly raising them. You could focus on the advantages of personalized service and offer guarantees and assurances that a giant conglomerate cannot match.

Disarm them with humor. Another strategy is to diffuse the situation with humor, especially self-deprecating humor. This can not only establish personal credibility with a less-than-receptive audience but it can also make you likable. President Reagan is most adept at deflecting criticism and antagonism in this way.

Disarm them with courage . . . and flattery! Appeal to your audience's innate sense of fairness and open-mindedness. Don't gloss over differences — acknowledge them. You might say, "Look, it's no secret that we have some disagreements over the best way to protect the environment. I honestly believe these are differences in approach and not commitment. I ask only that you listen and consider the possibility that another approach may be more effective. After my remarks, I'll be glad to stay as long as you like to answer your questions. I'll hear you out, which is only fair if you are willing to hear me out."

Each of these strategies requires a good understanding — in advance — of your audience and its convictions and concerns. Deciding which approaches to employ depends in large part on your assessment of the audience. If you are speaking to a blunt, cigar-chomping, seat-of-the-pants executive group, you might score points by getting down to business directly and being somewhat blunt yourself. In other cases, circumvention is more appropriate.

The key to the tough sell is to break down the barriers between you and the audience. This can be done with compelling arguments and a skillful performance. Through personalized touches, humor, and addressing the concerns you know are on the listeners' minds, you can get them to like and respect you as a person. They will then be more receptive to your message.

Being Booed — What a Joyous Experience!

The best way to handle a hostile audience is to know ahead of time that the possibility exists so that you can be prepared. But what happens if, to put it politely, your audience is a lost cause? What if, regardless of the approach you take, you aren't going to succeed in winning them over? In fact, you may even get booed!

Believe it or not, in some cases this can be beneficial and even enjoyable! I should know. I've been vigorously booed on a number of occasions.

During the presidential campaign of 1980, I was a surrogate speaker for Ronald Reagan in upstate New York. Among my unpleasant assignments: defend Ronald Reagan at a college forum alongside representatives of Jimmy Carter and John Anderson.

Unlike the 1984 campaign, the 1980 campaign found Reagan and his defenders hardly welcome on college campuses. Indeed, most student organizations viewed Carter and Anderson as too conservative for their tastes and instead endorsed fringe candidates like Barry Commoner. So you can imagine their receptivity to the likes of the actor from California!

I prepared for the worst — and I got it. Boos, catcalls, and hostile questions and comments filled the air of free academia. So resistant was most of the audience to my message that when I did strike home, they grew even angrier because I had challenged their preconceived notions.

For example, several questioners tried to establish the "fascist" credentials of Ronald Reagan. I pointed out that he was the only one of the three major candidates who opposed the draft and draft registration. The response? Groans of frustration that such a telling point had been made.

When they attacked Reagan's failure to endorse the Equal Rights Amendment that was currently before state legislatures, I

149

pointed out that obviously a president doesn't make a great difference since, during the entire four years of the Carter administration, not one additional state ratified the amendment.

The response again: groans, boos, and hisses, not at Carter or even at Reagan, but at me for scoring a point for which they had no immediate rebuttal.

And you call this fun?

Some people, myself included, actually enjoy the combat of politics and ideas. It's more pleasant if your audience will hear you out, then vigorously debate you. If this happens, settle back, ride it out, and have a good time!

More importantly, failure to impress one audience may greatly impress another. Courage and the daring to be different are prized qualities in our society. Standing up for your beliefs in the face of tremendous adversity can win friends in unexpected places.

For example, after I finished my rocky appearance at the college presidential forum, a number of people came up to me privately and expressed their admiration for my "courage." They felt sorry for me and admired the fact that I held my own. Several people also informed me that they intended to vote for Reagan. Peer pressure, often an important factor in audience (or is it mob?) psychology, kept them from speaking up.

The news media which covered the event also expressed admiration. The account in the local paper gave equal billing to my points as to those made on behalf of the other candidates — a courtesy that did not occur inside the auditorium. As a bonus, the reporter noted the difficulty of my task and the immature behavior of the audience.

You, too, should evaluate the success or failure of a particular speech along these lines. Regardless of the level of applause (or boos!) within the auditorium, did I get my message across to other equally important audiences beyond the auditorium?

Will the Real Audience
Please Stand Up?

This hostile-reception example demonstrates more than the possibility that such unpleasantries can bear important fruit. It also reminds us, when preparing a speech, that there may be more than one audience with more than one set of interests. It is your task to clearly delineate the audience most important to you, your organization, and the communications goals you have set. This determination will affect both the subjects you address and the manner in which you present yourself. Let's look at style first.

The most common dilemma for politicians is whether to cater their speaking styles to the live audience or to the much larger television audience. It is an important choice. With hundreds of the faithful before you, you may be tempted to whip the crowd into a frenzy with the most excitable rhetoric. The problem is, this may look awful on television, which doesn't take kindly to the huffing and puffing and ranting and raving of politicians.

Identifying your most important audience is critical to your choice of subject matter as well. In some cases, a speaker deliberately antagonizes a live audience. Why? Because he is playing to a wider audience — the media and its viewers — and he has determined that the boos of the former can win wild applause from the latter.

During the 1980 Republican presidential primaries, the candidates dutifully paraded before an audience of rabid New Hampshire gun owners to pledge their total allegiance to citizens' rights to keep and bear arms. All except one. John Anderson told the audience that he favored gun control. They practically shot him. Clearly he was a total bust in front of the several hundred hunters in the room.

But the national news media were in the room, too. They portrayed Anderson as a bold, courageous candidate who challenged voters' preconceived notions. Here, they said, was the candidate of vision and ideas.

151

Presumably, John Anderson anticipated the publicity value of being booed by gun owners. In this multi-media age, identifying your audience when you make a speech takes on a singular importance — especially in politics.

At times, the live audience often becomes little more than a prop for the wider media production. National political conventions are the most obvious examples. Not a single person in the room needs to be convinced of the virtues of the party, and barely a single convention-goer's mind will be or can be changed. Yet delegates' enthusiasm is used to generate excitement in voters' homes across the country.

Here are two more examples in which using a live audience as a prop for reaching a wider audience is to the speaker's advantage:

- A candidate is suffering from charges that he is in the pocket of organized labor and is not his own independent man. So he makes a speech before a labor group to tell them that in this competitive world, wage increases beyond the rate of inflation and productivity growth are a thing of the past. He still gets applause, he still maintains labor support, but he scores points in the media and the general public for being willing to deliver to his biggest boosters a tough, tell-em-what-they-don't-want-to-hear message.

- Another candidate is widely viewed as the candidate of big business. So where does he announce a get-tough policy toward industrial polluters? Not before environmentalists, whose skepticism and dissatisfaction are intransigent. Instead, he chooses a business group. Press reports: Candidate has the courage to challenge his own supporters to do better.

Executives in the business world should be equally cognizant of the potential and the pitfalls of multiple audiences. Before you approach any lectern to make a speech, you should ask yourself: "Who is listening?"

For example:

When you are making a speech to a civic organization and your chairman of the board reads an account in the newspaper, then in fact your speech may have been an audition for advancement as well as a talk to the civic group.

Or, let's say you talk tough to your division chiefs and employees about cutting costs and increasing productivity and many of them become resentful, does that mean your speech was a failure? Not if you were, at the same time, trying to send a reassuring message to your shareholders and board of directors!

Identify which audiences you want to reach and determine which one is the most important to you and your organization. Understanding the messages they respond to and the ones they block out will help you construct a message that will hit home.

Always Write It — Never Wing It

"Begin at the beginning and go on til you come to the end; then stop."

The King, in Lewis Carroll's
Alice in Wonderland

You've been through self-analysis in Step One and have been transformed into Sherlock Holmes in Step Two. Believe it or not, you're ready to begin your speech.

Well, almost. Let's review.

In Step One, I spoke of the need to be true to your purpose. Fulfill your assignment in a thorough, professional manner. Gaining this self-discipline is critical for good public speaking. Lacking it trips up many a bright performer. When your ego is in line, start giving it your all. Concentrate on every aspect of your appearance, presentation, and material.

In Step Two, I spoke of the importance of familiarizing yourself with your setting, of knowing the exact conditions under which you will be speaking. Topical research is important, but so are other preparations many speakers overlook. Investigate your audience. Make some basic strategic decisions about whom you want to reach and craft the presentation for their eyes and ears.

Now, you're ready to begin putting words to paper.

Let me say right off that I have violated and most likely will continue to violate the following admonition: *Always, always write out your speech before delivering it.*

Have you ever been to an important job interview, after which you repeatedly rerun the questions — and your answers — in your mind? And each time you do, you think of a slightly better answer than the one that emerged when it really counted?

Sound familiar? Perhaps at nerve-wracking interviews this can't be helped. But when it comes to speeches, second- and third-guessing should be done *before* giving the speech, not after. If you try to wing it, you may never reach the lofty altitudes of excellence. You may never even get off the ground.

Public relations executive and Reagan confidant Peter Hannaford is one of the nation's best speechwriters. He confirms my point. "Some speechmakers labor under the delusion that the only good speech is one given off the cuff. Even a masterful off-the-cuff speaker such as President Reagan knows this isn't true. I have been with him on countless occasions, before he became president, when he had to give seemingly extemporaneous remarks.

"They seemed that way, but I know that in nearly all cases, he was pulling them from his own memory bank. The phrases had a pace and conviction about them that brought immediate and positive responses, but they were not simply thought up on the spot."

What happens when you haven't adequately prepared your material? Hannaford relates one example of a speech by a government official. "Instead of speaking for twenty minutes — the ideal length — and taking questions for ten," he told me, "he spoke for forty minutes and took questions for twenty. He had a stack of notes and would pull from them, apparently at random, going off first in this direction and then in that. His speech was disconnected and his points unclear. It was an opportunity wasted."

With all the other preparations you undertake, and all that could be at stake, what could be more silly than leaving your speech to chance? After years of watching speakers fall flat on their behinds, including yours truly, I'm convinced that unless you are among a handful of brilliant performer/geniuses in the world, winging it is wrong.

Why do speakers insist on falling on their swords by attempting to speak off the cuff? Common excuses include:

- I don't have time to write out my speech. I know my subject, so why not just go up there and draw upon my expertise?

- I don't want to appear scripted. Colleagues will resent it that I've gone overboard to show them up by over- preparing just to please the boss. It looks like I've got it all together if I have the mental machismo to speak without notes.

- I like the freshness and the spontaneity of an off-the-cuff talk. And I like the rapport and eye contact I can develop with the audience when I don't have my nose buried in a text.

All of these are understandable concerns and sometimes good strategies for speech presentation. But implementing them should not deter one from full and complete preparation of the speech. All can be achieved without sacrificing preparation.

Expertise alone does not a good speaker make. Nor is a lack of time a good excuse for not fully preparing. If you don't have the time to devote to a speech, you shouldn't agree to do it.

As for relying on expertise in lieu of preparation: If you are an expert on your subject and the audience is not, your fund of knowledge may hinder you rather than help. I'm not saying that ignorance is a prerequisite for good speeches. But part of your preparation challenge comes in translating your technical knowledge into easily understood statements. You must find clear and simple ways of saying complicated things (more about that later). Unprepared, you are more likely to lapse into jargon and lose your audience.

Those who don't want to appear scripted make a good point. There are many situations where over-preparation could lead to excessive formality and stiffness, not to mention giving the impression that you couldn't survive without your five-by-seven cards.

The ascension of a former actor to the presidency has brought a new focus to speech preparation, because many of Reagan's opponents have advanced the idea that he is totally scripted and, indeed, superficial. One of Reagan's critics was once heard wondering aloud, "God help him if a stiff wind ever came up suddenly and blew away his speech cards. He'd be lost!"

Planning each thought and preparing a coherent speech does not mean you have to carry a script with you to the lectern. If you find yourself giving the same standard pitch frequently, you may find that bringing only notes or an outline will suffice. In this way, you can appear fresh and spontaneous. However, unless speech-making is old hat to you, not having a written-out text may produce exactly the opposite effect. At the first speck of trouble, you won't appear fresh and spontaneous, but scared and lost.

The "Spontaneity" of "uh" and "er"

Most people, when grasping for their next thought, almost unconsciously fill the void, however brief, with words like "and" or guttural sounds like "uh" and "er."

By writing out every word and then paring the speech down to its essential words, you can fine-tune not only content but also rhythm. President Reagan is known to have a habit of beginning sentences with the word "well," accompanied by a congenial tilt of the head. What is not generally known is that most of these "wells" are inserted formally into the text to provide him with a comfortable method of pacing his thoughts.

There are many occasions in which too much formality can make you and the audience uncomfortable. These forums include round-table discussions or speeches to small, informal groups. Solution: Totally prepare, but add an extra element to your preparation — memorization and the appearance of spontaneity.

The same goes for those occasions where you want the audience to believe you are such an accomplished expert that you can stand up on demand and make a brilliant speech.

I sometimes recommend that a speaker appearing before, say, a luncheon of fifty chief executive officers speak without notes. The corporate machismo culture regards speechmaking almost as an athletic event: It esteems individuals who can rise to the podium and belt out brilliance without having to "lean on" text. Fine, do it, I say, but first write out the speech and commit it to memory.

It is impossible to deny the lure of the off-the-cuff speech. When sitting in the audience at such an occasion, I hear comments all around me such as, "Wow, was he good — and he did it off the top of his head!" But if he truly did it off the top of his head rather than from memory, he took a big gamble. If you're lucky, you win big. If not, you lose. And in gambling, losers always outnumber winners.

For those tempted to ignore this pain-in-the-you-know-what advice, let's agree on this much:

- If you find yourself grasping for your next thought because you are under-prepared, it will show. The audience can tell that you really aren't sure what you are going to say next.

- It is possible to be overly formal and stiff in your presentation. The way to prevent this is not to prepare less but to prepare more. Work harder on being relaxed. Commit more of your speech to memory.

- Even though some audiences may be impressed by your seeming lack of script, you should never be embarrassed to take one to the lectern and read from it. If your performance is sufficiently polished, the audience will quickly forget all about it. You will appear scripted only if you seem unfamiliar with your text, not just because you have one.

- Don't push yourself to deliver speeches without a written text until you are ready. Don't go for the extra points until you have first scored the touchdown!

Handy, Readable Cards
Can Save Your Life!

I've practically begged you to write out your speech first. The next question is, what should you bring to the lectern?

I recommend a system used by California's governor, George Deukmejian. After he has finished work on a speech, he has it retyped in "orator" style print, which is larger than the capital letters on a normal typewriter. If you have access to an IBM Selectric typewriter, consider purchasing an "orator" typing element.

The governor has his speech prepared in this larger type, on four-by-six unlined index cards. The cards are numbered, and they are typed so that no sentence or paragraph is split between two cards. Several blank cards precede the typed ones so that he can jot down last-minute comments or acknowledgments during lunch or the introduction.

```
                        -4-

        HOLMES  LOOKED AT THE CONDUCTOR WITH SOME
    IRRITATION AND SAID, "THE PROBLEM IS NOT  WHERE
    MY  TICKET  IS.  THE  PROBLEM  IS  WHERE  AM I
    GOING?"
        THAT IS WHAT I WOULD LIKE TO DISCUSS WITH
    YOU  TODAY: WHERE OUR COMMUNITY COLLEGES SHOULD
    BE GOING, AND WHAT WE CAN  DO  TO  IMPROVE  THE
    QUALITY OF EDUCATION AT ALL LEVELS.
```

```
                        -5-

        OUR     ADMINISTRATION    STANDS     FOR
    OPPORTUNITY.  CALIFORNIA HAS A PROUD HISTORY OF
    LEADERSHIP   IN   OPENING   DOORS  FOR  PEOPLE,
    REGARDLESS  OF  THEIR  BACKGROUND.   I   HAVE
    DEDICATED MY  GOVERNORSHIP  TO  RESTORING THAT
    LEADERSHIP, AND WE BEGAN  BY  MAKING  EDUCATION
    OUR STATE'S HIGHEST BUDGET PRIORITY.
```

By typing your speech on index cards in large letters, you can improve your platform performance.

This system has several advantages. The text is unobtrusive to the audience. Even as we look forward to a speech, many of us have an innate concern with how long it is going to be. Watching a speaker carry to the podium a big notebook bulging with papers is quite disconcerting.

For men, cards carry the added bonus of fitting neatly into the side pocket of your suit coat. For women, they can easily fit into a handbag. Most speakers need both hands free right up to the moment of the speech for handshaking and back-slapping.

Many speeches immediately follow lunch or dinner. Index cards in the coat pocket or purse help keep your speech out of the salad dressing. And if you must write down a last-minute thought or make a change in your text, you'll have an easier time finding room on a crowded table for cards than for typewritten sheets.

Cards are also thick enough so that it is easy to move on to the next one without interrupting your delivery or rustling paper into the microphone. With a small amount of text per card, interrupted only at the end of a thought, you will experience less danger of losing your place. And, it is easier to make a sudden change to the middle of your speech by inserting a card where the new thought is supposed to go.

There are other effective systems, some of them rather clever. Don Kendall, former chairman and chief executive officer of PepsiCo, Inc., has his excellent speeches prepared on five-by- eight cards in extra large type produced by a special typewriter. The cards are hole-punched and bound together at the top with a plastic spindle. A small metal tab is fastened to each card, and the tabs are staggered. As Kendall delivers his speech, he feels for the tab on the card he is reading so that it's ready to flip over when the time comes.

Lacking such technology, most speakers will find four-by-six cards the best approach. (Avoid three-by-five cards. You can't get enough material on each card.)

One word of warning. Be sure you can read the type on the cards. Although you can see the type during a practice session when you are holding the cards six inches away from your glasses, what will you do if the practice conditions aren't duplicated on stage? The cards could be two feet from you there and the lighting might be poor. And if you are as vain as I am, you won't even want to wear your glasses.

For most, using orator type, or, at the very least, all upper-case letters, should suffice. By using cards rather than lined or roughly grained paper, you can enhance your vision of the speech as well. The amount of copy per card is limited. Sentences and paragraphs are undivided. With lines double-spaced and margins wide, you can ease the strain on your eyes, reduce the tension level, and devote full attention to superb delivery.

Recognizing that we are all pressed for time, I urge you to adopt as much of this advice as humanly possible. Sometimes attending to the small, technical details can make a world of difference.

As you gain experience, plotting out your words in advance and preparing your speech in a sensible format will come more quickly. With all the variables that determine success at the speaking lectern, it would be a shame to lose advantages that can be yours by taking a few practical steps.

Keep It Brief
(A Short Chapter)

"Be sincere; be brief; be seated."

Franklin Delano Roosevelt

Practice makes perfect, to coin a cliché you should never use in a speech. Let's "practice" the previous steps.

One: You've committed yourself to the speech, now commit yourself to some simple preparations — the words, the sound, the look, the enthusiasm. Be prepared to claim the immense power of speechmaking, but don't lose sight of the very practical, perhaps even mundane, reason you have been invited or delegated to make the remarks.

Two: To whom you say it and where you say it are as important as what you say. Identify the audiences you need to reach the most; learn enough about their likes and dislikes to plan strategically how you should deliver your message. Get comfortable with the physical setting of the speech by visiting the site before the big day. This way, you can put unknown fears out of your mind.

Three: Write out your material beforehand, every word. If the format calls for informality, write informality into your speech. If it calls for making a speech without notes, memorize it. Go to the podium free of opuses. Once you get behind the lectern and you're in the process of acknowledging applause, sneak your four-by-six cards out of your jacket pocket or purse.

Ready for Step Four? In the spirit of this lesson, I will try to keep this chapter brief. That's the step. Keep it brief.

The Ten Commandments are 297 words long. The Lord's Prayer is 56 words long. George Washington's second inaugural is 200 words long. Lincoln's Gettysburg Address is 226 words long.

By way of contrast, the U.S. Department of Agriculture's order on the price of cabbage is 15,629 words long.

167

I urge you to make your speech somewhere in between! Unless you have more wisdom to share than Lincoln, Washington, Jesus, or God, there is no good reason why you can't organize your material and deliver a persuasive, powerful message in twenty minutes.

Comedy writer Bob Orben has some advice when it comes to speech length. "You can't go wrong using the Richard Nixon approach to public speaking," he says. "First, write your speech, edit your speech, tighten your speech — then take another 18 1/2 minutes out of it!"

Communist leaders such as Leonid Brezhnev and Fidel Castro have been known to make speeches in excess of four hours. But who is going to complain? Who is going to walk out?

Most audiences, however, don't have to listen in rapt attention if they don't want to. Ours is a fast-paced society, a society on the move. Visual and aural stimuli are abundant. Information overload has set in. Thousands of ad agencies, politicians, community groups, entertainment media, and many others are competing for our scarce time.

By necessity and out of habit, the American attention span has shrunk. We want the news of the world in a half hour or less. The quicker the better. The same goes for entertainment. A show like *Miami Vice*, with its rapid sequence of visual images and fast-paced music, captures this new stylistic approach.

Simply listening to music is no longer enough for many fans. We want to "see" our favorite songs as well; hence, the popularity of music videos.

Remember when you felt "ripped off" if a movie was less than two hours long? Few of them were. Today, we get antsy and bored if a film is over two hours. Most clock in at around ninety minutes.

How many one-minute commercials have you seen recently? Thankfully, not many. Thirty-second and even fifteen-second "important messages" are the order of the day.

The speechmaker's dilemma is this: how to survive in a society that doesn't want to sit still, that is used to watching screens, not people, and whose attention span gets smaller every day?

The answer: Keep it brief. Keep it punchy. Keep it visual.

Dan Rather can do his thing in thirty minutes less commercials on the *CBS Evening News*. So can you. No matter how complex the subject or how detailed your knowledge, restrict a formal speech to no longer than twenty minutes.

The typical after-lunch-or-dinner speech to clubs or local organizations is ideally suited to a twenty-minute presentation. You should adhere to this time frame even if the organizer naively suggests he wants you to speak for forty-five minutes! At such functions, attendees usually are worried about time. They have to get back to the office or home to the babysitter. Maybe they have to go to the restroom after a big meal!

Keeping speeches brief challenges much of what we have learned in life, particularly the lesson that "more is better." Do you remember yourself as a student struggling to stretch book reports to meet the required five pages? Those who turned in ten pages always seemed to get A's. After a lifetime of conditioning to make things longer, no wonder it is now a challenge to make things shorter. Especially speeches. Keeping it brief is not easy. It may be the hardest part of writing your speech. We always think we have more impressive things to say than we really do. We believe every point is essential when it is not, that every word is critical when many could easily be removed. The problem is exacerbated when you are an expert on a subject trying to inform the uninformed.

What is the most significant point you want to get across? Do you really want or need to bring the audience up to your level of expertise? Certainly not. It is your goal to communicate some basic concepts and themes. With practice this can be done briefly. Remember the Ten Commandments!

What's the first step to successful speechmaking? That's right — speak with a strategy. This is also a valuable technique for helping you keep your speech brief. First determine your fundamental thesis. Once you are ready to put words on paper, try writing in capsule form this basic theme. Then build the speech around it.

How many words make a twenty-minute speech? That depends on how fast you read. Most speakers will cover one double-spaced typewritten page of material (approximately 250 words) in about two minutes. Therefore, a twenty-minute speech would consist of approximately 2,500 words — anywhere from seven to ten typed pages and approximately 30 four-by-six cards. But don't forget to leave a few minutes for applause and thank yous!

Rules Are Made to Be Broken!

Sometimes you will be required to break the twenty-minute rule. That's all right, I understand. Exceptions include:

● Making a presentation (for example, to co-workers at your company) which, due to the sheer volume of material you must cover, takes longer. When the boss says, give us an hour of ideas and proposals, you don't say, "Sorry, I never speak longer than twenty minutes!"

● Speaking to a class or other forum with an established time period longer than twenty minutes. If, for example, high school classes last forty-five minutes, students may get detention if they are released into the halls after twenty!

When yours is a command performance that requires longer presentations, there are a number of steps you can take to keep the pace flowing and interesting.

While I don't recommend visual aids for a typical twenty-minute speech (all eyes should be on you!), I do recommend them for longer performances. Charts, illustrations, exhibits, recordings, and even videotapes can keep the audience alert. So can audience participation, like a discussion or a question-and-answer period.

You should also consider a wider variety of stage movements. Change positions once in awhile. Move around the classroom or boardroom, if it's not too awkward. Breaking up your presentation with jokes, anecdotes, and examples — important in any speech (and discussed in Step Six) — becomes even more necessary in a longer speech.

If you are able to influence program planning, keep your speech brief. How do you squeeze in all the "truth" in just twenty minutes and still keep the audience impressed and entertained? If you're asking that question now, you're ready for Step Five!

Simplify Your Speech

"All writing is a process of elimination."

Martha Albrand

You may suspect that I'm beginning to contradict myself. I enticed you to these pages with the promise of the exhilarating power of holding an audience in the palm of your hands. But ever since, I have hemmed you in with rules and limits.

Don't speak too long. Don't stray too far from your topic. Don't neglect to fully prepare and write out your speech. Be sensitive to the needs and demands of your audience.

Now, the era of limits is over. It's time to learn how to unlock the tremendous power of spoken language.

I cannot teach you how to write in one chapter or even one book. It takes years of practice. But that's exactly what you've had — years of practice in conveying important messages to people important to you. That's what writing speeches is all about.

Translating Your Expertise into English

My job as a speechwriter entails translating the technical policies of state government into easily understood lay terms. Yes, I serve as kind of a translator, taking the language of bureaucrats and reshaping it into everyday English.

In one sense, my lack of expertise in most of the subjects about which I write speeches helps me rather than hinders me. When I call a policy expert for information, I receive answers that are often totally incomprehensible. I fuss and struggle with these well-intentioned people and coax from them explanations I can understand. Being a generalist prevents me from accepting their technical language and forces me to ask twenty questions and to suggest "translations" until the policy is understandable.

For example, when I hear this:

"DPA says authorized PYs are down except in Corrections, while OAL has promulgated fewer regs. We Lerped the budget year general fund and prioritized K-12 at the top. Revenues are up because the base is broader. The STIP is bigger than ever."

I translate it into this:

"We're spending more for public safety, education, and transportation by cutting bureaucracy and red tape and not by raising taxes."

Your challenge is the same. In most speeches, you will be talking to non-experts. You must take advantage of the respect they have for your expertise, while at the same time translate your technical knowledge into ordinary words to appeal to their general interest.

There are a thousand ways to say the same thing. Try to find the way to say it that is simple, clear, direct, and that appeals to the ear. Language is power, and if you use it properly you can make audiences believe and act upon what you are saying.

Can you do it? If you've got doubts, speech consultant John Connellan does not. He often bets his clients $50,000 that he can make them better public speakers in ten seconds. Here's how he explains it: "As soon as you leave here, I'm going to follow in an old beat-up Chevy and ram into the passenger side of your brand new Mercedes. I'll bet you are going to pop out of the driver's side and, in a very effective speech, tell everyone within hearing distance what you think of me and my actions."

His point is that most business people don't speak from the lectern as they do in real life. In most cases, during a speech, they become stiff, wooden, and lifeless. Strive to use everyday words that come naturally.

I suggest you begin the simplification process by writing a short paragraph or two containing the essence of your speech. I call it a speech capsule. It's not a detailed outline; that's easy. This challenge is more difficult: to express in the simplest terms the very essence of what you want to say.

For example, suppose you are an education expert and you've been asked to speak about the state of public education in America. Where to begin! There is so much you could say and so many facets to the topic.

After making some determinations about the audience and the event at which you will appear, ask yourself, what is the most important thing I want that audience to learn and remember?

You decide it's this: "All across this nation, in rich neighborhoods and poor, we are shortchanging our children with inadequate public schools, outdated curricula, poorly trained teachers, and campuses that are rife with drugs and vandalism."

Then you determine the best way to express your central theme, the most effective evidence to prove it, and what you want society and your audience to do about the situation.

In this case, your speech capsule looks like this:

Our nation was founded on *two* novel ideas, not just one. The first is that all men are created equal and that government ought to guarantee the individual's life, liberty, and pursuit of happiness.

The second idea is that universal public education was part and parcel of the democratic ideal, essential to the goal of equality and the happiness, productivity, and progress of each succeeding generation.

Today, we've neglected the time-honored ideals of the American past, and, in the process, we are handicapping the American future.

All across this nation, in rich neighborhoods and poor, we are shortchanging our children with inadequate public schools, outdated curricula, poorly trained teachers, and campuses that are rife with drugs and vandalism.

(Cite one example in each area, comparisons with the Japanese and West Germans, and statistics about declining test scores and rising drop-out rates.)

> We must reverse this downhill course before it's too late. Our children and grandchildren deserve better. How? Change must begin with you, the parents. Only when you start demanding a better performance from your kids and your schools, and a greater commitment from government policymakers, can we expect improvement.

Once you have developed a similar speech capsule, then focus on different ways to express and reinforce your basic ideas. Think about the make-up of your audience and devise lines of communication to them in the forms of comparisons, anecdotes, one-liners, and examples. Build bridges between your technical knowledge and the audience's general level of understanding.

Here are some guidelines to help you build those bridges:

SAY WHAT YOU MEAN IN SIMPLE, PRECISE SENTENCES. AVOID COMPLEX SENTENCE STRUCTURES WITH TOO MANY PHRASES.

Don't forget that the audience is not following along on paper. They're listening to you and hearing what you have to say for the first and only time.

Example: Translate this:

"Having said that, keeping in mind that we don't know whether the prime is still on a downward curve, the rate of permits and starts, seasonally adjusted, should continue to accelerate, barring any drastic deviation in current macro-economic policies."

Into this:

"Americans will build and buy more homes next year — as long as mortgage rates drop and the government sticks to its current policies."

AVOID JARGON, CLICHÉS, AND BUREAUCRATESE.

Translate this:

"EPA has line authority over Superfund, which means it impacts on which sites on the Superfund list will be prioritized. Fortunately, a spirit of bipartisanship has emerged on the Hill."

Into this:

"The Environmental Protection Agency controls the money for cleaning up toxics and decides which dumps will be cleaned up first. Washington agrees that toxic garbage should be kept clean of politics."

TALK IN PICTURES AND ACTION LANGUAGE.

Translate this:

"As we gather together today on this auspicious occasion, we begin a new era in the destiny of collective corporate challenge. With this dedication comes the determination to scale new heights of commerce and innovation, which we all know are critical to our future survival in the competitive global economy and as a force for good in our community."

Into this:

"Turning over this shovel of wet dirt today is just the beginning. Brick by brick, we're going to rebuild this company. We're going to rebuild this city, too. More business means more paychecks in the pockets of our workers and more pride in their hearts. It means more commerce bustling down the streets and avenues of this town and a better future for us all."

INTERSPERSE LONGER SENTENCES WITH SHORTER ONES TO AVOID MONOTONY AND ESTABLISH AN APPEALING, EAR-CATCHING RHYTHM.

Translate this:

"I believe America's best days are ahead. In the seventeenth century we first settled on America's shores. In the eighteenth century we fought a revolution and created a new nation. In the nineteenth century we tamed a wild continent and opened our doors to millions of immigrants. In this century, we became the world's greatest power and we landed on the moon. In the next century we will achieve even greater milestones."

Into this:

"I believe America's best days are ahead. And why not? We blazed three thousand miles of trails across a continent of wilderness, deserts, and swamps. But that's not all. We gave freedom a new home. We gave opportunity a new life. Is it any wonder that hopeful people from all corners of the globe are still beating a path to our door just as our ancestors did? America's past is a legacy of pride and prosperity. A promise of freedom and opportunity. In this century, we landed on the moon. In the next century, let's reach for the stars."

DON'T BE UNDULY CONSTRAINED BY THE STRICT RULES OF WRITTEN ENGLISH.

Peter Hannaford explains that: "People don't usually speak in sentences and paragraphs. So don't worry about making every sentence fit the precise rules of grammar. Pauses. Fragments. Run-ons. All are part of our speech patterns and can be very effective, provided they are used in a clear, purposeful manner."

Translate this:

"If you are willing to commit all your energies, resources, time, and expertise to this goal, then we are ready to do the same. It is evident that we cannot achieve success without your participation and your dedication. I am asking each one of you to make a decision today that will affect your future and that of your families for years to come."

Into this:

"If you're ready to make a commitment today, then so are we. We can't succeed without you. We need your talent and your energy. Your commitment and your support. How you respond will determine what kind of future awaits you. If that doesn't concern *you*, it concerns your children. And children are what this nation is all about."

WEED OUT DEAD WORDS.

Translate this:

"I happen to believe that our future will be bright if we can make some basic, important decisions in this year of great challenge, change, crisis, and debate. If we decide to pass on these decisions, or turn them over to the generation of Americans who follow us, then we can only predict that for the first time in the long, proud history of this bountiful society, the America our children will know will be poorer, not greater, than the America which you and I were so very blessed to know."

Into this:

"Our future will be bright if we meet the challenges facing us. If we fail, our children and grandchildren will pay a severe price. For the first time, a new American generation will have fewer opportunities than its parents."

At the outset, fully applying these guidelines may take editing and re-editing. I suggest that after you write your speech, examine it critically. Apply these tests:

- Is the speech simple and clear?

- Does it capture the natural rhythms of your speech?

- Does it convey concrete picture images as opposed to vapory concepts?

181

- Is it enjoyable to listen to? Is the flow catchy and entertaining?

- Are the sentences direct and uncomplicated?

- Are there any dead words or incomprehensible terms?

- Does your speech sound like you and say what you want said?

Think of yourself as a sculptor of words, molding each point you wish to make in the most communicable, entertaining, and natural ways you know. One useful exercise may be to talk out what you want to say. Put it in your own words, off the top of your head to a friend or into a tape recorder. You'd be surprised at the clarity and eloquence of your comments before the pressure of putting them down on paper begins to intimidate you.

Be vivid. Be clear. Be direct. Be natural. If you follow these rules, your speech will be persuasive and powerful.

A Private Peek at a Master at Work

Love him or hate him, few would disagree that Ronald Reagan has an unparalleled ability to communicate with the public. A key to his strength is an ability to turn the complex into the simple (some would say simplistic) and to talk in word pictures that average people can grasp and understand.

Like other busy politicians, Reagan employs speechwriters. They're the best in the business. But it is interesting to see what the Great Communicator does to the work of a Great Speechwriter before the speech reaches its final form.

The speech excerpted below was ultimately delivered at the annual meeting of the U.S. Chamber of Commerce in April, 1982. Here are some examples of the metamorphosis of the speech after President Reagan reviewed and edited it. As you read sections from the two versions, notice how the president made a good speech better by applying some of the guidelines outlined in this chapter. (A facsimile of the entire document is included in Appendix One.)

Speechwriter's draft: The Chamber is celebrating an important milestone this week. You've almost caught up to me — almost, but not quite. From one who has been there already, may I just say: you're not getting older, but you sure are getting better. I never thought I'd be able to say this, but I've found something that can grow faster than the Federal Government — the membership of the Chamber of Commerce of the United States — and that makes me feel mighty good about our future.

Reagan draft: The Chamber is celebrating an important milestone this week. Your 70th anniversary. I remember the day you started. Like good wine, you've grown better, not older. The membership of the Chamber of Commerce of the United States is the only thing that's grown faster than the Federal Government. Thank heaven!

Speechwriter's draft: Well, if I could make a suggestion, our Administration still has a small problem on Capitol Hill we would love to have your help on.

Reagan draft: Well, if I could make a suggestion, our Administration has a few small unfinished problems — about $400 billion worth — on Capitol Hill we would love to have your help on.

Speechwriter's draft: I happen to believe Thomas Jefferson was no reactionary, but a true progressive when he warned:

Reagan draft: Thomas Jefferson was no reactionary. He was a true progressive when he warned:

Speechwriter's draft: We will never abandon our commitment to the needy.

Reagan draft: We are meeting our commitment to the needy even if that hasn't been the subject of a network documentary.

Speechwriter's draft: Yes, we have compassion for the needy. But how about a little compassion left over for the group Washington so often forgets — the wage earners and taxpayers of America? They are the heart and soul of the free enterprise system: They pay America's bills, they have been burned by higher inflation and taxes year after year, and they need help.

Reagan draft: We are the most generous people on earth. I don't think any of us lack compassion for the needy. But isn't it time we had some compassion for those unsung heroes who work and pay their taxes and their bills while they struggle to make ends meet? They are the heart and soul of the free enterprise system. They need help too.

Speechwriter's draft: If it's commerce, they regulate it. If it's income, they tax it. If it's a budget, they bust it. Given their way, they'd make everything that isn't prohibited — compulsory.

Reagan draft: We can no longer listen to those who say if it's commerce, regulate it. If it's income, tax it. If it's a budget, bust it. Given their way, they'd make everything that isn't prohibited — compulsory. Well, a better rule is — if it ain't broke, don't fix it.

Speechwriter's draft: Just as important, we preserve one of the few systems left on earth where people at the bottom of the heap can reach for the stars, and I still believe that's what America should be all about. From now on, more of what people earn belongs to them. The age of redistribution and erosion of freedom must end. We will reclaim our freedom; we will create wealth again; we will not retreat from the historic reforms and increase the tax burden upon the American people.

Reagan draft: Just as important, we preserve one of the few systems left on earth where people at the bottom of the ladder can still get rich. That's what America should be all about. From now on, more of what people earn belongs to them. (Rest of paragraph deleted by the president.)

With his editing pencil, the president has adhered to many of the basic rules we've been discussing. He weeded out unnecessary words and made sentences shorter. He composed paragraphs in a sing-song kind of rhythm. He translated big words and complicated sentences into the American vernacular. He employed examples, humor, and analogies to make his points. He forcefully asserted his beliefs without trailing off into abstract concepts.

Remember, you've got just one brief shot at an audience. You're talking from a text you have written, rewritten, and rehearsed. The audience is hearing your words for the first time. Your use of simple, clear, attention-grabbing language is one of the most important ingredients of a successful speech.

Your goal is to have the audience remember and appreciate your central theme, act upon it, hold a high opinion of you and your organization. It doesn't matter whether they remember *everything* you said.

Today's public speaking requires other ingredients as well. One of the most difficult to add is the mysterious spice called humor. That's the subject of Step Six.

Add Humor

"Next to being witty yourself, the best thing is being able to quote another's wit."

Christian N. Bovee

I've got some bad news for you, and I feel it is my duty to break it to you before we go any further.

Your question: Am I expected to be funny in my speech?

My answer: Yes.

Let's face it, we have a fetish for the funny. We like to laugh and expect to be amused, even in otherwise thoroughly depressing situations.

Even grisly murder movies or violent cops-and-robbers shows are expected to have humorous situations and funny characters. Not to mention more than a dozen James Bond movies. Laughing in the face of death is an integral and time-honored part of our culture. When we sit before a stage, we expect to be entertained. Boredom and deadly seriousness are cardinal sins.

So here we are as public speakers, non-comedians under great pressure to be funny. The therapy of some guides is to comfort you by saying that you don't have to be funny, witty, or entertaining in your speeches. I believe you must be. Audiences expect it, and humor is one of the best ways to communicate your themes, viewpoints, and positive aspects of your personality.

I have had accomplished speakers tell me quite frankly that the only part of the task they fear is the fear of not being funny. Even worse: the fear of trying to be funny and falling flat. I can assure you that when I am assigned to write a speech, coming up with a witty one-liner or amusing anecdote is the hardest part of my job. In some cases, assuming I'm familiar with the subject, I can write a fifteen-minute talk in an hour and a half — a half hour to write the speech and an hour to find that perfect joke!

On more than one occasion, politicians and corporate board chairmen have called me in total anxiety minutes before a speech because they don't have a joke to tell. For many people, being funny clearly is the most harrowing part of public speaking.

And here I am, supposedly building up your confidence by telling you that you have to be an entertainer on stage!

A Bob Hope Joke-writer Has Some Advice for You

Having possibly scared you to death, let me take some of the fear out of joke-telling with a few suggestions.

Doug Gamble, a Los Angeles-based humorist, has written humorous material for Bob Hope, Ronald Reagan, and many other entertainers and politicians. He's a natural, one of the best. I talked to him recently about the role of humor in speeches:

"I think the use of humor in speeches and public appearances is becoming more and more important," Gamble told me. "We live in a society where audiences expect to be entertained as well as informed. But beyond the entertainment value of humor, we're seeing it used more and more to make points or reinforce ideas.

"For example, President Reagan told an audience during the '84 campaign that the Democrats' call for a tax increase is their typical knee-jerk reaction, and 'every time their knee jerks, you get kicked.' The line got a big laugh but also underscored the president's opposition to tax increases. It wasn't a joke for the sake of a joke, but one that made a point."

I asked Gamble why audiences seem to insist on humor, even when serious topics are being addressed.

"The simple answer," he said, "is that people enjoy hearing something that makes them laugh. But also, I think we generally feel more comfortable around someone who demonstrates a sense of humor, someone who breaks the ice by generating laughter in the audience.

"An audience won't necessarily relate to everything that is said in a speech, but virtually everyone in the audience will relate to something that's funny. Humor can serve as an instant connection between the speaker and the audience. And humor can be used even when serious topics are addressed because most people don't feel entirely comfortable with a speaker who takes himself or his subject too seriously."

What qualities does humor reveal in a speaker that are important to convey to the audience? Gamble replies:

"A speaker who uses humor is a speaker who wants to establish a quick rapport with the audience, something the audience usually appreciates. A speaker who uses humor (uses it effectively, that is) will probably be liked by the audience even before he gets to the heart of his message. Humor reveals in the speaker the fact that he cares about his audience and cares about his subject.

"It seems one of the personality traits we most value in others is a sense of humor. In fact, one of the worst things you can say about a person is that he doesn't have one."

Okay, Doug, you convinced us of the necessity for humor. Now, tell us how to be funny!

"The best source of humorous material for the speaker who can't come up with his own is a professional joke-writer. (Hint! hint!)

"Seriously, the kind of humor I most like to use myself and most enjoy writing for others is self-deprecating humor. I also think it's the type that can be used most successfully. People like people who can poke fun at their shortcomings. It goes a long way to getting them on your side by proving that you don't take yourself too seriously.

"When a speaker uses self-deprecating humor, he is revealing confidence in his own abilities. He's letting the audience know that he is *so* self-assured, he can readily poke fun at himself.

"President Reagan has used self-deprecating humor very effectively. When Walter Mondale accused him of 'government by amnesia,' the President said, 'I thought that remark accusing me of having amnesia was uncalled for. I just wish I could remember who said it.'

191

"When it was reported that he fell asleep at inopportune times, he said, 'With so many hot spots around the world, I've told my aides that whenever they hear of trouble they should wake me up immediately — even when I'm in a cabinet meeting.'

"Governor Deukmejian uses a line in some of his speeches in which he tells the audience, 'I understand that you have been searching for a speaker who can dazzle you with his charm, wit, and personality. I'm pleased to be filling in while the search continues.'

"By using this line, he has turned a disadvantage into an advantage. Instead of the audience sitting there and thinking that he's not a very exciting speaker, the listeners are on his side, laughing along with him.

"Another very successful kind of humor is the humor that reinforces a point. I wrote a line for a U.S. senator once who was making a speech on the high cost of medical care. He said, 'I went to the doctor yesterday with a sore throat, and he told me to come back when I had something more expensive.' It amused the audience and reinforced the senator's theme."

Drawing upon Gamble's advice, I have summarized the ways in which humor can effectively improve your presentation:

Use humor to break the ice with the audience. When you first get up to speak, the audience is still in the process of looking you over. Perhaps they're finishing dessert and adjusting themselves in their chairs. The beginning is a critical time to establish that you are confident and in charge. Since you can't say, "Shut up and listen," you can quickly capture their attention with a joke or a humorous comment. You will score points instantly, and a once-restless audience will look intrigued, anxious to hear what else you have to say.

What should you be funny about? The humor should be natural and appropriate to the situation. For example, don't say, "Before I start, I heard a good one the other day." First of all, the audience may not agree that it's a good one; but, more importantly, when you so blatantly try to establish yourself as a joke-teller, the same audience that expects to be entertained could quickly become an audience that resents you for wasting its time.

Perhaps there is humor to be found in relating your situation to the news of the day. Several years ago, Governor Deukmejian told an audience, "My battles with the Legislature have grown so fierce that when I turned on the news the other day, at first I couldn't tell whether they were talking about Lebanon or the State Capitol."

Another common source of opening humor is your profession (or that of the audience). If you are a lawyer talking to other lawyers, make a joke or wisecrack about lawyers. Don't worry that some of them may have heard it before. If it's good, they'll laugh anyway.

One tactic is to use as a source of humor a well-known person on the dais or in the audience who is notorious for some particular style or activity. By all means, don't make the Rotary Club president the butt of all your jokes! But, when properly used, this approach can be effective.

Another great source of ice-breaking humor is so obvious it is staring us right in the face. Make a joke about making the speech.

One effective technique used by Governor Deukmejian, a big fan of brief speeches, is to start by saying, "I don't plan to speak very long today," followed by a wisecrack about why not.

There are many, such as:

"Winston Churchill once said there are only two things more difficult than giving a speech after lunch. Climbing a fence that's leaning towards you — or kissing a pretty girl who's leaning away from you."

"Thomas Jefferson once said, 'It is the trade of lawyers to question everything, yield nothing, and talk by the hour.' I'll try to resist that tendency today."

"I'll start talking and I assume you'll start listening. But if you finish before I do, I'll understand."

"They tell the story about the long-winded senator who traveled thousands of miles from Washington to his home state to witness a hanging. When they asked the condemned man if he had any last words before the hanging, he said no. The senator said, 'Then, sir, would you please yield your time to me?' And the condemned man said, 'Sure. As long as they hang me first!'"

Use occasional jokes or one-liners to break up the text. Sometimes even the best speeches need that extra jolt of energy or shift in gears that can best be produced by a witty one-liner or a funny joke.

Witticisms, anecdotes, and humorous examples change the pace. Try to include these in your presentation in a natural way that's appropriate to your topic. Again, don't say, "By the way, I heard a story the other day . . . ." Gratuitous jokes totally unrelated to the subject at hand do not serve your purpose. Weave any joke or anecdote into the flow of your thoughts.

Here are a few examples:

You are speaking to the local PTA about the need for better schools. You say, "I have just outlined some of the problems facing our schools. There are many. But let's be thankful that we don't teach our kids the way the Russians teach theirs. When a student asked his teacher why the shelves in the Soviet Union are so empty while the ones in America are so full, the teacher put it this way: 'In Capitalist countries,' he said, 'workers don't earn enough money and so store shelves remain full. It is the buying power of the Russian comrades that keeps our stores empty!'"

Perhaps you are talking about agriculture: "So many of our friends and neighbors are going under. Things have gotten so bad that when one farmer recently won a million-dollar lottery, he was asked how he planned to spend the money. He said, 'I'm just going to keep on farming until it's all gone.'"

By finding these clever ways to make your points, you can more effectively communicate, particularly in the body of your text. That's when you run the greatest risk of losing your audiences to their own private thoughts about washing the car or walking the dog.

Humor, examples, and anecdotes can re-energize you and the audience and reinforce your major themes.

Use humor to deflect criticism or singe opponents. Politicians on the hot seat often find humor an effective tool to extinguish the critics and singe opponents. With humor, you can deflect concerns and develop attack themes against your opponents while avoiding the harshness of a frontal assault.

For example, Abraham Lincoln once said, "I've been told I was on the road to hell, but I had no idea it was just a mile away with a dome on top!"

President Reagan is particularly adept at this kind of humor. As we saw in the Chamber of Commerce speech discussed in the last chapter, Reagan deflects concerns about his age by joking about it. This technique came to full fruition in the second nationally televised debate in the presidential election of 1984 when Reagan, as mentioned earlier, sealed his reelection on the power of a single funny line about his opponent's youthful inexperience.

Humor can also be used to put down adversaries, but be sure to do it with a smile. Walter Mondale's "Where's the beef?" attack on Gary Hart turned the contest around for the 1984 Democratic presidential nomination. During the general election campaign, we were treated to such gems by Mr. Reagan as, "I would say that Mr. Mondale is starting to tax my patience, but I don't want to give him any more ideas."

Some laughs are too expensive. One kind of humor I don't like involves references to the audience's boredom or to your travail, real or imagined. Self-deprecating humor at the beginning of the speech is one thing. It serves to lower expectations so that when you are terrific, the audience is that much more impressed. But during your talk, comments such as, "For those of you who are still awake" or "Don't worry, this oratorical version of *War and Peace* is almost over," are depressing acknowledgments that you view the speech as a chore or that the audience may find it unpleasant to sit there and listen to you.

195

Once you are into the body of a text, the world you create in the speech should take on a life of its own. No more references about the speechmaking process, good or bad. Even if you are doing a less than thrilling job, "it ain't over til it's over," as Yogi Berra says. Your conclusion may still knock 'em dead.

Of course, you'll knock yourself dead if you resort to humor with even the slightest tinge of ethnicity. Avoid ethnic jokes and offensive humor at all costs. It's important to develop a sensitivity to humor you may enjoy but others find demeaning. Before telling a joke, examine it critically for ethnic, racial, religious, and sexist content. If you have the slightest doubt about whether it is appropriate, don't tell it, or get a second or third opinion.

Where to Find Humorous Material?

In addition to acting on Doug Gamble's "hint" to hire a good joke-writer, you can also develop your own original material. You'd be surprised at how much of the world's daily goings-on are downright funny, if not hilarious. Scan the newspapers and news shows for material that fits your topic. Sunday newspapers, which are usually loaded with feature columns and enticing tidbits of humor, are a good source. So are weekly news magazines, entertainment publications, and the *Reader's Digest*. You may also get ideas from Johnny Carson, Bob Hope, and other speakers. Above all, when you hear something funny that fits into your speech, steal it!

If you've already heard some of the one-liners and jokes I used as examples in this chapter, that's no accident. I didn't make up a single one of them myself. Very few jokes are original. Have you ever met the author of a joke? Mostly, you meet people who are retelling a joke, perhaps with a few embellishments or local variations. No one really knows where they begin.

Even professional joke-writers and comedians rely primarily on variations of familiar and basic themes. If you hear a good line, unless it was specifically commissioned for someone else and paid for, you should not hesitate to use it. It has become part of the public domain.

Other useful sources for humorous and anecdotal material are the many anthologies published to help public speakers. I recommend these within limits. They can be helpful, but primarily for giving you basic ideas for entertaining material. Don't plan on using the lines word for word. Take the basic idea and twist it and change it to more appropriately relate to your subject. The Appendix includes a list of some of the anthologies I feel are most useful.

When Not to Be Funny

As a general rule, audiences expect humor and anecdotes. Humor helps you communicate and them understand. It makes them more receptive to your message. It breaks down barriers that all the passion, determination, and fiery oratory sometimes can't demolish.

Still, there are occasions where humor is inappropriate. Obviously, if you are laying a Memorial Day wreath at the town monument to fallen soldiers, jokes are uncalled for. The same goes for funerals — well, most funerals. On other occasions, humor must be handled more deftly, almost covertly.

For example, if you are called before the corporate brass to make a presentation, you don't want to give the impression that you are managing your assignment frivolously or that you are a smart aleck who doesn't take the task seriously. Nevertheless, you can deliver an effective speech in a wry, witty, and clever way, humoring the boss without appearing grim or squandering his time.

When I speak of "humor" I am not necessarily referring to side-splitting belly laughs. Witty comments, clever analogies, and humorous asides will draw chuckles and smiles of understanding. These spicy touches can make your speech come alive!

197

What If No One Laughs?

It has happened to the best. It will happen to you. You tell a joke. It might be the funniest joke in the world. But maybe someone in the front row sneezed and drowned out your punch line.

What's funny is extremely subjective. It depends on who's doing the listening and who's doing the telling. This is one reason I recommend one-liners, wry comments, and humorous examples rather than hard-to-tell, complicated stories that require loud guffaws from the audience in order to be deemed successful.

If a one-liner falls flat, it is easy to forge on without too much embarrassment. But if you invest the time and effort to deliver a five-minute knee-slapper and no one laughs, the humiliation is acute.

What do you do when you tell one that's not funny? Be funny about not being funny! Johnny Carson has perfected this fallback. When a Carson line falls flat, he cracks a new joke about the fact that he has just told a bad one.

Try it yourself. If you get a few snickers or half-hearted laughs, that's good enough to escape the situation. Simply plunge on. Don't even acknowledge your less-than-spectacular success. Just don't use the joke again. But if you really bomb, just look up and say, "Hm, and to think Bob Hope gave me that one himself!"

Create a Fireworks Finale

"Speak properly, and in as few words as you can, but always plainly; for the end of speech is not ostentation, but to be understood."

William Penn

You've been preparing your speech with care and diligence. You've made sure you fully understand the event and the audience. You're prepared to write out your speech. You've settled on your theme and you've been drafting the language to convey it. You've risen to the necessary challenge of being humorous and entertaining. Now, let's discuss one more essential element of the speech before we put all the ingredients together.

Composing a Fireworks Finale

A significant theme of *Winning Them Over* is the imperative to pay homage to the needs and habits of the modern audience. In the television age, we are accustomed to receiving our information in quick, enticing, and entertaining tidbit images.

Yet thanks to the time-honored traditions of the past, a speech is still a place where you can let the eloquent rhetoric soar. Most audiences will allow you a few minutes of fanciful flowing words, particularly as you conclude your presentation.

You begin with the necessary thank yous and acknowledgments. This is important. It establishes you as gracious and grateful. Then, you break the ice with humor, skillfully disarming the audience with your wit. Next, you get into the meat of your text, establishing a quick pace, yet a comfortable flow. The audience is interested. You keep them guessing; you keep them from settling back in the comfort or discomfort of their chairs. You deliver your message in a unique and intriguing way, deliberately breaking up the delivery with flashes of humor.

But by the end of your twenty minutes, you turn dead serious. You have one last opportunity to win them over. A chance to pull it all together. To be profound and moving.

Eloquent endings are old-fashioned, but I like them and I believe audiences do, too. It's almost as if, for a few brief moments, they escape from the stressful demands of our high-pressure world and welcome your gifts: insightful vision, persuasive rhetoric, a touch of philosophy, a little emotion, and, yes, even a hint of corniness.

Many speakers use the conclusion as an occasion to quote great leaders or scholars. Others do this throughout the speech. That's fine if the quote perfectly fits the material. But if it is gratuitous, or if your great philosopher is too obscure, the audience will be unmoved.

There are a number of handy quotation books, a few of which are listed in Appendix Two. But may I make a suggestion? Instead of relying on the great quotes of others, dare to write your own. Write your conclusion so magnificently that you become quotable in your own right.

Above all else, avoid limp endings such as:

"Well, I see our time is almost up, so let me conclude by saying . . . "

Or this:

"Let me summarize . . . "

Or this:

"With that, I'd like to thank you for your attention and also thank the chamber for giving me this opportunity to be here today." (Do your thanking at the beginning. By the end of your speech, all the thank yous should be coming in *your* direction.)

I must also advise against concluding with a joke or humorous story. It trivializes your presentation at a time when it should be the most compelling.

Instead, achieve a command performance. Execute your finale in a crescendo of passion and conviction. Summarize, but do so unobtrusively, with eloquence and heartfelt emotion. Sensing the conclusion, the audience will make every effort to let you convince them.

One effective conclusion is to share a glimpse of the future — a bright future that can be had if the audience follows your advice. Let's consider an example. Suppose, as director of a regional commission to improve public education and resolve delinquency problems, you have just unveiled a program for educational reform. Rather than conclude like this:

"So to sum up, I believe we'll meet these challenges if you'll join me in supporting higher salaries for teachers, new curriculum development and review, minimum graduation requirements, and stricter policies for dealing with campus violence, drug use, and vandalism. I would appreciate your support for these measures. Thank you very much."

Try impressing your listeners with a stunning finale like this:

"Ladies and gentlemen, I come before you not only as an educational commissioner but as a concerned parent.

"President John F. Kennedy once said, 'A child mis-educated is a child lost.'

"Let's not lose any more of our children to hopelessness and mediocrity. Let's teach our children to say yes to reading, writing, and arithmetic — and to say no to drugs, delinquency, and dropping out.

"I want our kids to have the best public education in the state and I know you want that, too.

"I want every child to ride to school in a safe bus. To enter a classroom where the teacher cares and has time to care.

"And in the lunchroom, shouldn't the topic of discussion be the latest flavor of ice cream rather than the latest designer drug?

"If we continue arguing among ourselves, our children will continue to lose. But if we join together, a united team, then I know we can give our kids the hopeful future they so richly deserve."

203

I'll give you a moment to wipe the tears from your eyes!

Now let's combine all the ingredients we've been discussing into one proven recipe for a great speech:

I. Thank Yous and Acknowledgments

There's no need to go overboard and flatter your audience, but some nice words about the sponsors and their projects show that you appreciate the opportunity you have been given, that you care about them, and that you have taken the time to learn about them. (1 minute)

II. Ice-breaking Humor

Try a self-deprecating comment or a joke about not speaking too long or some humor about the news of the day. This will reassure the audience and establish a quick rapport and receptivity. (1 minute)

III. Statement of Purpose

Begin with a broad overview statement that sets out your basic themes and goals for the speech. I believe this is best done by relating an anecdote or personal example rather than proclaiming an outline. Instead of this:

"Today, I'd like to discuss four measures pending before the city council, and then I'll make some comments about alternatives. Finally, I'll give you some ideas on what you can do to help."

Try this:

"Today, I had the opportunity to attend my sixth-grader's class play, and seeing the hopeful, enthusiastic faces of those children reminded me once again how important it is that we meet some critical challenges facing our city today." (3 minutes)

IV. Speech Body

Deliver the meat of your speech in several segments of approximately three minutes each, broken up by one-liners or humorous examples. Construct simple, clear paragraphs, interspersing short and longer sentences. Speak in language that is natural and direct, rather than technical and bureaucratic. (12 minutes)

V. Soaring Summation

The time for humor, frivolity, and detail work is over. It's time to sum up without saying you're summing up. Soar to a conclusion that thematically reinforces your major points in an uplifting way. Quote a great leader or admired hero if you feel the quote is appropriate. (3 minutes)

Total: Twenty minutes. Oh, I left out time for one thing — thunderous applause!

This is not meant to be an airtight structure but rather a loose guide for those new at speechwriting and speechmaking. Sample speech openings and conclusions are presented in Appendix Four.

Shifting Gears
Without Grinding the Clutch

Flow. That's a persistent challenge in speeches. We have spoken of the need to use language that flows along natural rhythms of speech and conversation. Don't talk like a robot. Instead, talk like the next-door neighbor. Flow is also a problem when you have to weave a number of sometimes very diverse thoughts and topics into one coherent whole.

Try to avoid laborious transitions, such as numbering your points. I don't know about you, but when a speaker tells me at the outset that "there are four issues I'd like to discuss," I become more conscious of time. I look at my watch. I perform a mental "countdown" of the points.

Also, try to avoid other stodgy mechanisms such as "on another subject," or "let me turn to another point." There are better ways to let the audience know you are moving on.

The best transitional device, of course, is the burst of applause! Try to cap off one discussion with a compelling, lectern-thumping summary line. The audience's applause will provide a natural breaking point, and, as it stops, you simply start discussing the next subject.

How do you write applause lines into your speech? A million bucks to the person who can guarantee it! Audiences often are conditioned not to interrupt a speaker with applause even when they love what they are hearing. This is especially true of professional audiences but not as true of political ones. If you determine that you are speaking to an audience with the potential to applaud throughout the speech, treat the closing lines of each theme as a kind of emotional coda.

Example: You're talking about crime to a community group. You mention some programs, laws, budgets, and procedures that should all help the crime-fighting effort. At the end of that discussion, you go to the gut issue: tapping the fear of crime and the resentment of criminals that most people possess. You say: "With these new laws we're going to close the loopholes in our criminal justice system. We're going to get the hoodlums off our streets and put them behind bars where they belong — and when they get there, I think they ought to work and earn their keep just like the rest of us."

Humor, followed hopefully by laughter, also serves as a good breaking point in which you can raise a new subject. Yet, for most speakers, relying on humor or applause for topical transitions is risky. I suggest you write thematic transitions into your text. Think of a common thread that binds the two topics, even if only tangentially.

Suppose you are speaking on education and you want to turn to the economy. Begin the new subject like this: "Education is fundamental to opportunity. So is creating enough jobs for our growing population."

Or perhaps your topic is the economy and you want to shift to a discussion of your company's philanthropic activities. Try something like this: "As our economy surges ahead, we must ensure that no one is left behind."

If you are speaking about your company's expansion plans and you want to turn to a discussion of drug abuse prevention in the community, you can try another technique: accentuate rather than obscure the transition to achieve a dramatic effect and the rapt attention of the audience.

It might go something like this: "Now, I had originally planned to end my remarks right there, but I don't think any responsible person can talk about the future of our community without discussing a modern-day plague which could end that future and all that we have worked for: drug abuse among our children."

As you can see, there are a number of things you can do to make a smooth transition; however, in most cases, just a simple line connecting your themes, nothing too cute or contrived, can keep your speech flowing effortlessly to a triumphant conclusion!

Don't Be Afraid
To Be Afraid

"Cultivate ease and naturalness. Have all your powers under command. Take possession of yourself, as in this way only can you take possession of your audience."

Charles Reade

The big day is here. You've studied, written, prepared, and practiced to the hilt. How come you're still nervous?

Maybe you haven't prepared properly. Maybe nervousness is just plain natural.

Unfortunately, I have no magical solution to the tensions of speechmaking. You may have been told to single out a person in the audience and look him in the eye, pretending that instead of making a speech you are chatting pleasantly with a friend.

I don't like this technique. Have you ever been the audience member singled out? I have, and I hate it! If a speaker maintains consistent eye contact with me in a crowd of hundreds, I get extremely uncomfortable and look away, which may be even more disconcerting to the speaker.

Usually, people are scared for two reasons. They're afraid of the unknown, and they're on edge when something really important is at stake.

Fear of the unknown won't be problematical if you properly prepare. Preparation removes as many unknowns from your presentation as possible.

As for the other kind of fear, this is natural and even useful unless carried to an extreme. If you become a bundle of raw, jagged nerves, if you begin to jabber or shake uncontrollably, the audience will notice and feel uncomfortable and sorry for you.

But being on edge, with your adrenalin flowing, means you are ready and rarin' to go. Instead of feeling fearful, get excited. Remember, if you've prepared the way I've suggested, you have nothing to worry about that is within your control. You'll pass. You'll get by. You won't blow it. Now your challenge is to make the grade of A.

You can reduce your nervousness and rechannel it into productive energy, not just through preparation but through preparation and practice according to a sensible timetable:

Three Days Out

Don't wait until the last minute to prepare. One of the surest ways to heighten tension is to wait until the day of the speech to call the sponsor for information or to stay up late the night before your speech frantically writing and rewriting. Make sure your speech is done several days in advance.

This doesn't mean that you have to treat your speech text like a stone tablet. If a brainstorm strikes the night before and you think of a one-liner or an additional illustration, by all means, make room for it. But by preparing several days in advance, you can relieve the pressure and minimize the disruptions in your normal daily routine.

Two Days Out

Rather than setting aside big chunks of time for preparation on this day and working yourself up in formal practice sessions, fill your free moments with a quick read-through of your cards. Become familiar with your speech. Make it fit like a comfortable old shoe.

One Day Out

It's time to get a little more serious and formal in your preparations. Reserve some time in the day to rehearse. Practice not only the speech text, but also its delivery, including facial expressions and body movements.

How best to rehearse? I'm not keen on practicing in front of a mirror or before a handful of friends or co-workers. These simulations do little to approximate the actual speech situation. On the contrary, I find them inhibiting, embarrassing, and sometimes more nerve-wracking than the actual speech!

The fact is that you are not going to deliver your speech to your three best friends but to a room filled with people. I recommend quiet time by yourself, reading your speech aloud at the volume you will read it the next day. Talking it out is essential. You must determine if what looks good to the eye sounds good to the ear. Are sentences simple and short enough so that you have time to catch your breath at natural places? Are there any impossible tongue twisters which should be changed?

With this kind of practice, you'll find that in a relatively short period of time the most natural and appropriate facial expressions, vocal inflections, and human emotions will come forth.

You may have noticed that I have not prescribed any clever system for marking your text with underlines or other notations such as happy faces telling you when to smile. To me, these indicate a lack of preparation. Rather than facilitate delivery, they lead to unnatural and exaggerated expressions.

On stage, as you are delivering your speech, such reminders to smile, be forceful, or be hushed will distract you. They'll make you think about that particular gesture and become self-conscious about it. Why not practice sufficiently beforehand so that all these movements and emotions flow naturally?

One last point about the day before . . . .A good night's sleep instead of a raucous party won't do you any harm!

Morning of the Speech

Pay special attention to your grooming. If there's a day when it pays to put every hair in place, this is it. Choose your outfit carefully. Clothing is a very personal matter, and you have a lifetime of experience in dressing yourself! Wear colors and styles that are right for you, clothing which makes you feel comfortable and confident. Nonetheless, a few general guidelines apply to both men and women, similar to those we discussed in Part One:

- Avoid extremely dark or extremely light outfits. Clothing should be dignified without being too somber.

213

- Avoid gaudy displays, such as dangling earrings, shiny bracelets, "loud" ties, or flowery handkerchiefs. You should strive for an expensive, substantial look, but not an ostentatious one.

- Unless the event has a special dress code (such as for a company retreat or picnic), men should refrain from sport coats and women from pantsuits. Dress appropriately for the occasion, then up it one notch. Your goal is to stand out without sticking out.

Women executives find that they must take special care when dressing for speeches and presentations. Regrettably, some prejudices still exist against women in business and professional occupations. Your entire demeanor, including your wardrobe, may be judged more harshly than that of men. If your outfit is too becoming, if it shows too much bosom or leg, the audience, both men and women, will be put off. You could appear frivolous. On the other hand, you could be criticized if your outfit looks too masculine.

Women executives know better than I the special and often unfair circumstances they must confront. You have probably made your peace with an unfair world long before you picked up this book or you wouldn't be an executive in the first place. You have already established your business world *modus operandi*.

Men and women both, your outfit will not be complete until you take a few simple precautions. Keep a kleenex or handkerchief handy. The only thing more embarrassing than blowing your nose on stage is having to do it without a handkerchief!

Place some cough drops or throat lozenges in your pocket as well — even if you're feeling fine. Tension or a hot auditorium can close the throat, dry it out, and cause a tickle or even a coughing fit. And, just in case you miscalculated your vision needs on that podium, carry your eyeglasses with you, too.

At the Event

Leave enough time so that you don't arrive out of breath and perspiring. Remember, all eyes will be upon you the moment you enter the room. Conduct yourself as if the speech had already begun, in a confident, relaxed, and self-assured manner.

During the events leading up to your appearance, pay attention! Be prepared to jot down additional introductory notes as other speakers take the platform or as announcements are made. This demonstrates that you are really part of the event and the sponsoring group. If you are sitting at an elevated head table, remember that the audience may be watching you throughout the program. So watch how you eat and try to stifle those yawns! If you are an after-lunch or after-dinner speaker, also watch how *much* you eat. Indigestion and oratory don't mix!

I remember the first speech I ever wrote for a leading corporate executive. He made the mistake of eating a salad with heavy garlic dressing right before he got up to speak. He told me later it was like trying to talk with a mouthful of cotton balls.

On the Platform

After you have been introduced, smile and proceed to the podium confidently. Look like you know who you are and what you're doing. Give the audience a moment to get settled. Stand up straight, but not stiffly. Unless you are there to sell rings and watches, don't drape your arms over the lectern; keep them at shoulder's width, gently resting your hands on the lectern inset. As the applause dies down, unobtrusively remove your speech cards from your pocket or bag and place them in front of you.

I don't like to see a speaker remove his watch and set it in front of him. The audience sees this. It makes them conscious of time and indicates that you aren't sure how long your message is. That means you aren't sure *what* your message is.

How you utilize your voice is important, too. Like many other people, I tend to talk through my nose and could be one of the prime beneficiaries of some voice lessons. Train yourself to speak from your chest rather than your head. Keep your voice in its lower ranges.

215

Microphones distort everything in the upper ranges. Learn to breathe with your diaphragm and vibrate the air in your chest. Try not to let the air and the sound go through your nose.

A Few Words about Gestures and Movements . . . .

Other speech guides emphasize elaborate systems of body pivots and hand gestures. The problem is that, unless you are an accomplished stage actor, these prescriptions will very likely make you more self-conscious and wooden in your performance.

One speaker I know was told to smile more in speeches. Now she smiles too much and at the wrong times. Another was told to move and make eye contact with all sides of the audience rather than just stare straight ahead. Now, like a human metronome, he speaks with his head swaying mechanically back and forth, back and forth.

Be relaxed. Be natural. Most of us do not speak with our arms locked at our sides. Neither do we gesture with every sentence. Move your hands gracefully or forcefully on occasion but don't let them do the talking. Let your arms fall gently back to the lectern.

Staring straight ahead means ignoring two thirds of your audience — which you want to avoid by all means! But don't become locked into a monotonous rhythm where left, right, and center each receive alternating stares of fifteen seconds. Mix it up a little.

All the world is a stage and you're on it. Master it. Let confidence and the precision of your speech be reflected naturally in your movements on stage. Pause for effect when you want. Raise and lower your voice when it feels right to so do. Relax. You're prepared, polished, and ready. It is going to be so much easier than you ever imagined!

After the Speech

You've worked hard for this day, so by all means bask in the glow of your applause. Make your move off the stage back to your seat. Try not to look too impressed or smug about your smashing success. Stick around, answer questions if members of the audience approach you. Get their feedback. Welcome their comments with grace and pleasure.

216

Have I proposed too many recommendations for the busy executive to handle? While immersed in these chapters, you might feel that way. But most of these steps are easily accomplished and in time will become almost second nature.

You don't need to drop all your activities for days at a time in order to make a successful speech. Spread out over a number of days, these preparations take very little time. You run a much greater risk of disrupting your routine when you leave your speech preparations to the last day. Weave them into your daily schedule and they will barely distract you.

Triumph Over Adversity

"Speak clearly, if you speak at all; Carve every word before you let it fall."

Oliver Wendell Holmes

The keys to effective speechmaking are confidence, preparation, and predictability. With these assets, you are in control. Without them, anything goes.

I've emphasized the role of total preparation and the elimination of unknowns to build up your natural self-assurance as a go-getter. But let me also urge you to retain an element of flexibility in your speech presentation so that you can respond to things that aren't in the script.

I have already alluded to some of the possible grenades which could be thrown at you during the course of a speech. Let's review these and introduce some others, along with possible responses.

Your joke doesn't get a laugh.

If you receive mild chuckles, smile and charge on. At least you reached a few diehards during one of the speech's most challenging moments. If absolutely no one laughs, try a joke about not being funny. In all cases, do your best not to become flustered and red in the face. Forge on. Keep your composure. In a moment, it will all be forgotten.

If you have a heckler.

Turn that nuisance into a blessing. Don't get angry. The audience will be on your side. Make a funny comment such as, "Is there an echo in here?" or calmly say that you wish that everyone could respect the rights of others to hear and be heard. The audience will likely signal its unanimous agreement with applause.

221

The public address system breaks down.

Nothing is more aggravating to speaker and audience than ear-splitting feedback or a microphone that doesn't work. If this happens, don't fuss and fumble yourself with lame comments such as, "Is this working?" Calmly turn to the host and say, "If some of you are having trouble hearing me, I'd like to pause until the problem is corrected." Unless the problem isn't going to be corrected, wait until the situation has been attended to.

You have a coughing fit on stage.

If you get something caught in your throat, turn away from the microphone and clear your throat. Calmly take a sip of water, and resume by saying "excuse me" and continue.

If the problem becomes really bad, pause as long as you have to. Make sure the problem is solved before you start again. One long, embarrassing coughing fit is better than three. Then, make a comment to diffuse the embarrassment such as, "Losing my voice may be the luckiest thing that's happened to you in a long time!"

The audience is obviously bored and unresponsive.

Don't make comments like: "Is anyone still awake out there?" or acknowledge your less-than-spectacular reception in any way. Try picking up the pace of your delivery, deftly changing the level of your voice. Continue to do a professional job. Don't cut corners. You may not be wowing them, but you can maintain your dignity. Even if the audience is underwhelmed, most will respect you for doing your duty. They will leave knowing you made a sincere effort.

The program changes unexpectedly.

Recently I was asked to speak before a civic organization. I was warned by the sponsors that it would be a long program and that I would be the third of three keynote speakers. Accordingly, I kept my prepared remarks to ten minutes. Yet at the luncheon, there were not three, but six speakers! And I was last!

As speaker after speaker droned on, many of them striking the same themes, the audience grew restless and bored. Children frolicked in the space between the podium and the dining area. Soon a steady trickle of people flowed out of the banquet hall. By the time it was my turn, half the audience was gone, and the speeches alone had been going on for an hour and a half.

I realized there was no way I would deliver my full remarks. So I had to perform a feat that is somewhat equivalent to talking and chewing gum at the same time — I had to edit my remarks as I was standing at the lectern reading them!

Thorough knowledge of my text sure came in handy. As I completed each paragraph, I noticed that one corner of my mind was anticipating the next one and determining if it could be cut. I ended up delivering a five-minute talk instead of a ten-minute one. The beleaguered audience seemed appreciative.

Even under these trying circumstances, I did get interrupted by applause once. It was at the beginning. I shouldn't have done it, but I couldn't resist it. Some awards had been given out earlier in the program. I said, "I think the real award should go to the audience for listening to all these speeches!"

The moral of this story is to be prepared to adjust your remarks to changing or unexpected circumstances. A lengthy program is one situation where on-the-spot editing is necessary. Another is a change in the weather. I recently addressed an outdoor graduation ceremony. Just as I was getting into the heart of my speech, I felt the pitter-patter of raindrops on my head. The sky was on the verge of opening up, and I had ten minutes to go! Once again, I edited my remarks as I delivered them. Familiarity with my text made this possible as well as a sure knowledge of my essential points.

Often circumstances may dictate sudden changes in *your* text. There are occasions when previous speakers tell the same joke or quote the same statesman. Sometimes a prior speaker makes a statement you disagree with and you want to correct the record. If you can do this without discarding your central purpose or running over your allotted time, then do it. Your ability to react with flexibility to these situations can make the difference between success and failure.

223

Beware of question-and-answer sessions.

Giving the audience the chance to ask questions after your speech should always be cleared and arranged in advance with the host. You should be aware of both the advantages and the pitfalls. Your carefully developed thesis could fall victim to an off-the-wall question — or answer! If you are being covered by the news media, something you say in response to a question may interest them more than your speech, and that could become the news of the day.

The problem is not so much being stumped by a question as it is surrendering the tight control and predictability you aimed for in planning and polishing your presentation.

Still, points can be scored by taking questions after a speech. Doing so involves the audience and dispels any doubts that you are but a scripted robot that can't think on its feet. It establishes a unique rapport with the audience. And, it gives you an opportunity to immediately gauge the initial reaction to your speech.

I recommend question-and-answer sessions when the audience is relatively small, when the format is informal, or when the time allotted you is unusually long. I discourage them if the audience is large. There is nothing more clumsy and aggravating for both speaker and audience than trying to take questions from either the front or the back row of a huge auditorium. You will almost always have to repeat the questions before answering them.

When you agree to answer questions you agree to the possibility of receiving hostile questions or commentary which challenge your facts and conclusions. Don't be afraid or defensive! Respond as best you can with conviction and certainty, not with anger or emotion. Be polite, respect your challenger's right to disagree, but stick up sincerely for your point of view.

There are no perfect solutions to the unfortunate occurrences that can mar a speech. But if you are relaxed, confident, and flexible, you can learn to respond well to difficult situations. Don't lose your cool. Don't get flustered. Respond with grace and ease. If you try to pretend nothing is wrong, the audience will leave wondering whether you really know what's going on around you.

By being on stage, you are in command. Take charge of un-foreseen circumstances in a professional, but not overbearing, way. When difficult moments are handled with skill and self-assurance, you will further demonstrate the leadership qualities you set out to display in the first place. When it comes down to it, leadership is the real topic of every speech.

Win Them Over!

"Be a craftsman in speech that thou mayest be strong, for the strength of one is the tongue, and speech is mightier than all fighting."

Ptahhotep, 3400 B.C.

Let me share with you a speechwriter's tall tale. It's about a hard-driving senator, a real, well, for lack of a nastier term, SOB.

This senator was terrible to his staff, particularly his speechwriter. On one occasion, he called the poor soul into his office on Friday afternoon at five o'clock and said, "Here's a famous quote I want to use in my speech on Monday morning. But I need to know who said it. Find out by then or you're fired."

The speechwriter worked all weekend. He read books of quotations from front to back. He spent Saturday night at the Library of Congress. No luck.

Forty-eight hours later, he humbled himself before the senator. "I'm sorry, sir, I can't find this quote anywhere."

The senator smiled. "Good. I'm the one who thought of it. But before I used it I just wanted to make sure no one else said it before me!"

But the speechwriter got even. He knew the senator was the kind of guy who didn't follow any of the rules when it comes to speeches. One day, the boss was in a mad rush. He called the speechwriter in and said, "I've got to make a speech on energy on the Senate floor in one hour. Give me a twenty-point energy plan and a compelling speech by then. Bring it to me down on the floor."

The speechwriter did just that. With no time to review, the senator grabbed the sheets and got up before his colleagues and the national press. He began to read: "Today, I am pleased to announce a twenty-point plan to free this great nation from the clutches of foreign oil dependency. Let me now outline my program."

He turned the page. Instead of twenty points, all it said was, "Okay, you SOB, you're on your own!"

Preparation: It makes all the difference. I'm not talking about hours of drudgery. I'm talking about making all things which can be known known. Preparation means following some easy steps in a logical fashion.

I have found that other books on public speaking substitute pep talk for straight talk, anecdotes for practical advice. Perhaps the authors assume that by saying over and over again, "You can do it," they can make you, the reader, believe it.

I, too, believe confidence is essential. But confidence as a speaker is not gained by simply wishing it to be true. It comes from experience. It comes from preparation. It comes from having a practical, step-by-step plan of action.

Here is that plan:

Step One: Speak with a Strategy

Every time you speak, you must be true to two topics. The first topic is the one you've been asked to speak about. The second topic is leadership. View every speech as an exciting experience, a chance for you to exhibit your persuasive powers and your leadership potential. But don't consider it an opportunity to cut loose from the specific task you have been asked to perform. Stick to your first topic, and the second — your capacity for leadership — will shine through.

Step Two: Spy on Your Audience and Setting

A speech is a social act, not a monologue delivered to the bathroom mirror. In order to effectively communicate, you must not only understand your subject matter but your audience as well. What audiences do you want to reach — the people inside the room, the news media covering the speech, a particular boss or VIP in the group, the general public? What kind of message does your chosen audience understand?

What is the physical setting for your speech? What is the exact nature of the program in which you are participating? How long are

230

you expected to talk? Will there be a lectern to your liking available? Will you be able to read your text under these conditions?

Step Three: Always Write It — Never Wing It

An effective speech requires that every thought be fully fleshed out and put in precise language before you get up on stage. Length, timing, rhythm, coherency — all require writing out a speech in advance.

If you wish to speak from notes or memory, you should still plot out your entire speech in advance and memorize it.

For the smart speakers who talk from a text, use big type on four-by-six unlined index cards, numbered and bound together by a rubber band. Don't break up a sentence or a thought between two cards — you will be less likely to lose your place when reading.

Step Four: Keep It Brief

Whenever you have influence over the program format, keep your speech to twenty minutes. If yours is a "command performance" where a longer presentation is required, be sure to break it up with visual aids, discussion, questions and answers, and entertaining material.

Today's audiences will not tolerate lengthy, dry speeches. Editing down is a key challenge in the speechwriting process — a valuable exercise that will inspire you to present only the most important thoughts and themes.

Steps Five, Six, and Seven: Simplicity, Humor, and Eloquence

Your twenty-minute presentation is best structured as follows (see Appendix Four for sample speech openings and conclusions):

1. Open by graciously thanking your hosts and the audience for the opportunity to speak.

2. Break the ice and establish rapport with a joke or a humorous comment.

3. Begin with a thematic statement of your topic and your purpose.

4. Deliver the key segments of your message using simple, clear, direct sentences that are written for the ear, not for the eye. Employ examples, illustrations, and analogies. Avoid dead words, bureaucratic lingo, and vapory concepts. Be natural, be down-to-earth, be direct. Change the pace every several minutes with a humorous one-liner, example, or joke; but be sure these relate in some way to the subject at hand.

5. Conclude your speech by restating your basic themes, but in a dramatic, uplifting tone, not that of a legal brief. There is still a place for beautiful rhetoric in speeches — at the end.

Step Eight: Don't Be Afraid to Be Afraid

Remember these simple rules for an effective speech performance.

1. Don't be afraid to be afraid. Instead, channel your nervousness into determination to win them over.

2. Minimize raw fear by writing and preparing your speech at a relaxed pace, well in advance. Don't psych yourself out by doing everything the night before or by locking yourself away days before the speech. If you plan in advance, you can prepare in a relaxed way that does not consume too much time or disrupt your normal schedule.

3. One to two days before the event, practice your speech by reading aloud from your speech cards in the calm and quiet of your home or office.

4. Get a good night's sleep before the day of the speech. On the morning of your speech, pay special attention to your grooming.

Wear clothing that expresses dignity and substance, nothing too somber or frivolous. Avoid gaudy displays of jewelry and other accessories.

5. Approach the podium with confidence and good cheer, not with fear and lockjaw. Stand up straight but not stiffly, keep your arms by your side, and speak from your chest, not through your nose. Establish eye contact with all sections of the audience — left, right, and center. But do so naturally, not mechanically: You don't want to appear like a robot!

Step Nine: Triumph Over Adversity

Your careful preparations and eliminations of unknowns can't prevent the unpreventable such as a coughing fit, a broken microphone, a heckler, a joke fallen flat, or an audience unimpressed. There are specific steps you can take to minimize these problems and to diffuse them. The important lesson is that you do. Don't plunge on as if nothing were happening. Acknowledge the problem, take action, or ask that action be taken. Demonstrate leadership skills, display grace under pressure, and carry on.

Step Ten: Win Them Over!

You've known how to communicate since the day you were born when you screamed and hollered your little lungs out for a bottle.

Since then, your skills have grown and changed in a thousand ways. So has society and its demands on communicators. If you can keep up with these fast-changing communication demands, you will be successful in your field and in society.

I've often said that a field like mine, speechwriting, is one of the truly unnecessary careers in modern society. Why? Because the men and women I write speeches for all have the potential to be great communicators on their own. If they had the self-assurance or the time to craft their own speeches, they could communicate with the public much better than I.

You don't get this far by being incapable of communicating with your family, friends, neighbors, superiors, and underlings. You've got tremendous talent and a great potential for leadership. By following the easy steps in this book, you can effectively persuade, charm, and lead through speechmaking.

I have tried to offer a way to structure the talent you already have, to channel it to produce an effective presentation. There's nothing to fear if you are prepared. A speech should make you no more or less nervous than any other important business or professional activity.

Let me confess something. Until I began to write this book, I never realized I had a particular method or replicable technique for communicating through the press or through speeches. I resisted the idea of writing this book because I wasn't aware I had a system. After I thought about it, I realized I did.

The same goes for the many experts in the field of communications whom I consulted for this book. As one put it, "What is my system? I don't have a system. I just write speeches."

I am often asked who are the best speakers I've heard or seen. We're aware of the great speeches of historical figures such as Lincoln, but only by reading them in textbooks. When I think of great speakers, I think immediately of Ronald Reagan and the late Dr. Martin Luther King. They differ greatly in style, not to mention substance. But both mastered the art of communicating publicly. Both inspire me, from a craftsman's point of view, when I hear their speeches.

I hesitate to say it, but some of the greatest speakers have also been among mankind's most evil leaders. Hitler mesmerized a nation with his oratory. Divorce yourself from his message of hate, and who could deny that Louis Farrakhan is a speaker of tremendous ability? So was the Reverend Jim Jones.

Communications is power, at times beneficial, at times destructive. The power to persuade, the power to move a mass of people from one position to another. The power to get others to do what you say and believe what you think.

Some say that great oratory is dead. It's a relic of a past era. Nonsense. The tyrants of the world don't believe it. It's time that the constructive forces, representing the voices of freedom, democracy, and positive human progress, learned the same lesson.

All the rules and guidelines in the world can't replace the fact that to be successful as a speaker, you must find your own voice, using language that is right for you. You must have something meaningful to say and know what you are talking about. You must believe in what you say. You must feel confident in what you believe.

There are few things more precious than the opportunity to share hopes, dreams, wishes, concerns, and fears with your fellow citizens. Use this privilege well; use it wisely. Give it the strength of your deepest convictions and the commitment of your hardest work. If you learn to do it well, you will be successful. You will rise in your chosen field to a powerful position of leadership and make an important contribution to your organization and to society. You will open a vast range of spectacular opportunities for the future. You will win them over!

The Final Step:
Choose Success Over
Standing Still

Throughout the ten strategies and ten steps of *Winning Them Over*, I have proposed concrete, pragmatic actions to improve your communications skills — skills that can help turn you into a leader in your organization and your field. But I've saved the most important step for last: **Choose success over standing still!**

If you remember that communications is the key and employ the relatively simple approaches in this book, you will find that this is one of the easiest choices you will ever make.

Yet, sadly, many professionals with great potential don't make that choice. Bright, capable, and dedicated people excel in substance but flunk out when it comes to communicating their creativity and realizing their leadership potential.

Remember our tale of two executives? Bill Warner, now on top of his world, could have been a John Harper, toiling anonymously in the bowels of the organization — and vice versa. The theme of this book is that capable, talented people like Bill and John, like you and me, can choose between success and standing still.

Let me say that some individuals have leadership potential but nonetheless are perfectly content to play behind-the-scenes roles. It is their privilege to make that choice. But it is a *choice*.

If you want to make the other choice, however — the winning choice — begin by implementing the strategies and steps in this book.

Now that you've nearly completed *Winning Them Over*, you know what it's all about. Let me tell you now what it's *not* about. It is not about how to manipulate the media and spread falsehoods to the public. This book is for those who believe in the truth as they sincerely see it and who want to share their ideas and convictions with the community.

In the hands of people who lie, the power to persuade is dangerous and destructive. But put that power in the hands of individuals who want to make a positive difference — not only for themselves but for society as a whole — that's the essence of a successful democracy.

Communications, through speeches, presentations, and dealing with the press, is not public relations fluff. It need not be exercised at the expense of substance or principle.

A good communicator is simply recognizing social reality. We don't live in a vacuum. We make our mark in life and our contributions to society not only by having good ideas, solid achievements, and strong principles but by sharing them with others as well. The way we do that in the 20th-soon-to-be-21st-century is through public speaking and the mass media.

As a speechwriter and communications professional, I am sometimes asked how I feel *I* am making my mark in life. After all, they say, I'm not inventing products, contributing to substantive policy, or providing the public with needed services. i'm simply promoting an image.

My answer goes something like this: If an individual is not a successful communicator, growing and adapting to rapidly changing media technology, he or she won't be a successful leader. So, I work for leaders I believe in and agree with, hopefully helping them to be better communicators and thus better leaders. The more skillfully I do my job, the more I can see my beliefs and my principles translated into action in the marketplace of American democracy and free enterprise.

The same goes for you. If you believe in something strongly, you aren't compromising your principles by learning how to sell it. You are meeting your social responsibility by making an effective contribution. And if you strongly believe in success, you have the responsibility to yourself, your family, and your community to make it happen.

You *can* make it happen by filling the human stage with your bold, confident, and persuasive presence. If leadership beckons to you, don't back out. If success appeals to you, then choose it. Step up to center stage. Turn your ideas and talents into action. Win them over!

Footnotes

A Tale of Two Executives:

1. Gerald J. Voros and Paul Alvarez, *What Happens in Public Relations?* New York: AMACOM, 1981, pp. 3-6.
2. Lee Iacocca and William Novak, *Iacocca, An Autobiography.* New York: Bantam, pp. 71-72.
3. Jeff and Marie Blyskal, *PR: How the Public Relations Industry Writes the News.* New York: William Morrow, 1985, p.169.
4. Blyskal, p.168.
5. Voros and Alvarez, p 12.
6. Blyskal, p. 10.
7. Blyskal, p.28.

Strategy One:

1. Richard A. Snyder, "Can We Trust the Big Media?" *Vital Speeches*, January 1, 1985, pp.174-75.
2. Peter D. Hannaford, *Talking Back to the Media.* New York: Facts on File Publications, 1986, p.12.
3. J.F. Cooper, *The American Democrat.* Cited in George Seldes, *The Great Quotations.* New York: Lyle Stuart, 1960.
4. Hannaford, p.28.
5. Jack W. Germond and Jules Witcover, *Wake Us When It's Over.* New York: MacMillan, 1985, p.9.
6. Stanley Rothman and S. Robert Lichter, "Media Versus Business." *Current*, January, 1983, p.38.
7. Hannaford, p.22.
8. Cited in James J. Kilpatrick, "Monthly Column." *Nation's Business*, March, 1985.
9. Hannaford, p. 25.
10. Hannaford, p. 26.
11. Fred Barnes, "Media Realignment." *New Republic*, May 6, 1985, p.12.
12. Barnes, p. 14.
13. "Behind Wave of Libel Suits Hitting Nation's Press." *U.S. News and World Report,* November 5, 1984, p. 53.

14. Hannaford, p. 11.

15. Jody Powell, *The Other Side of the Story*. New York: William Morrow & Co., Inc., 1984, pp. 14-15.

16. Hannaford, p. 21.

17. Leonard Downie, *The New Muckrakers*. New York: New American Library, 1976, p. 278.

18. Susan Miller, "The Young and the Restless." *Washington Journalism Review*, October, 1985.

19. Hannaford, p. 19.

20. Kilpatrick.

Strategy Two:

1. Rothman and Lichter, p. 38.

2. Dorothy Lorant, "Can We Talk?" *Washington Journalism Review*, July, 1985, p. 47.

3. Lorant, p. 47.

4. Hannaford, p. 93.

5. Lorant, p. 48.

6. Powell, p. 300.

7. Lorant, pp. 47-48.

8. Philip C. Smith, "The Will to Win." *Vital Speeches*, February 15, 1983, p. 267.

Strategy Three:

1. Blyskal, pp. 28, 48.

2. Blyskal, pp. 51, 60.

3. Voros and Alvarez, pp. 44-45.

4. Voros and Alvarez, p. 41.

5. Voros and Alvarez, p. 53.

6. Voros and Alvarez, p. 41.

Strategy Six:

1. Evans Witt, "Here, There, and Everywhere: Where Americans Get Their News." *Public Opinion*, August/September, 1983, p. 46. Hannaford, p. 50.

Strategy Eight:

1. Voros and Alvarez, pp. 47-48.
2. George Marotta, "Op-ed Article Excellent Outlet." *Media Resource Guide*. Los Angeles: Foundation for American Communications, 1983, pp. 28-29. This guide contains much useful information on many of the media approaches discussed in Strategy Eight.
3. Gene Fuson, "How to Use Broadcast Editorials." *Media Resource Guide*, pp. 32-33.

Bibliography

Blyskal, Jeff and Marie Blyskal. *PR: How the Public Relations Industry Writes the News*. New York: William Morrow, 1985.

Blythin, Evan and Larry A. Samovar. *Communicating Effectively on Television*. Belmont, Calif.: Wadsworth, 1985.

Cannon, Lou. *Reagan*. New York: G. P. Putnam's Sons, 1982.

Chambers, Wicke and Spring Asher, *TV PR, How to Promote Yourself, Your Product, Your Service, or Your Organization on Television*. Rocklin, Calif.: Prima Publishing, 1987.

Detz, Joan. *How to Write and Give a Speech*. New York: St. Martin's Press, 1984.

Downie, Leonard. *The New Muckrakers*. New York: New American Library, 1976.

Germond, Jack J. and Jules Witcover. *Wake Us When It's Over*. New York: Macmillan, 1985.

Hannaford, Peter D. *Talking Back to the Media*. New York: Facts on File, 1986.

Harris, Morgan. *How to Make News and Influence People*. New York: TAB Books, 1976.

Howard, Carole. *On Deadline: Managing Media Relations*. White Plains, New York: Longman, 1985.

Iacocca, Lee and William Novak, *Iacocca: An Autobiography*. New York: Bantam, 1986.

Lant, Jeffrey. *The Unabashed Self-Promoter's Guide*. Cambridge, Mass.: JLA Publications, 1983.

Peters, Thomas J. and Robert M. Waterman, Jr. *In Search of Excellence*. New York: Warner Books, 1982.

Powell, Jody. *The Other Side of the Story*. New York: William Morrow, 1984.

Prochnow, Herbert V. and Herbert V. Prochnow Jr. *The Public Speakers Treasure Chest*. New York: Harper & Row, 1986.

Quinlan, Joseph. *Industrial Publicity*. New York: Van Nostrand Reinhold, 1983.

Ross, Mitchell S. *The Literary Politicians*. Garden City, N.Y.: Doubleday, 1978.

Spicer, Keith. *Winging It: Everybody's Guide to Making Speeches Fly Without Notes*. Garden City, N.Y.: Doubleday, 1982.

Valenti, Jack. *Speak Up With Confidence: How to Prepare, Learn, and Deliver Effective Speeches*. New York: William Morrow, 1982.

Voros, Gerald J. and Paul Alvarez. *What Happens in Public Relations?* New York: AMACOM, 1981.

Appendix One:
President Reagan at Work

The following is a full reproduction of a speech by President Ronald Reagan to the U.S. Chamber of Commerce in April, 1982. The typed draft was presented to the president by his speechwriting staff. The handwritten changes and additions are the president's. A discussion of this speech is contained in Part Two, Step Five.

(Elliott/AB)
April 22, 1982
2:30 p.m.

CHAMBER OF COMMERCE 70TH ANNUAL MEETING
APRIL 26, 1982

Thank you very much and good morning to you all. Don

Kendall, I have a hunch you knew exactly what you were doing:

First the patriotic music, then your inspiring speech, then that

great film and what do you know -- we've all caught that Pepsi

spirit. Don Kendall is a powerful spokesman ~~and I think he's~~ (FoR FREE ENTERPRISE)

~~been one heck of~~ a chairman *as he's a 10.*

Well, this is a happy day, and I am honored to be with you.

~~Your group, I can tell you, is not only close to my heart, but~~

You have earned the great respect of individuals and

organizations all across this country *and may I say a ~~few~~ warm*
spot in my heart.

~~I couldn't help noticing~~ The Chamber is celebrating an

important milestone this week~~.~~ *~~You've almost caught up to me --~~*
~~you think. This goes even ~~ ~~you ~~ ~~with about~~
~~almost, but not quite. From one who has been there already, may~~
~~I just say: you're not getting much older, you sure are getting~~
~~better. I never thought I'd be able to say this, but I've found~~
~~something that can grow faster than the Federal Government~~ -- the

membership of the Chamber of Commerce of the United States -- and

~~that makes me feel mighty good about our future.~~

Great organizations don't just happen. They are built by

strong leaders with vision and determination to reach a greater

good. Back in 1975, such a leader arrived at the National

Chamber. He came with a sense of history, an understanding of

the economy, a belief in America and her future. For 2 days he

huddled with his new staff, working out your statement of

Page 2

mission: "To advance human progress through an economic,
political, and social system based on individual freedom,
incentive, initiative, opportunity and responsibility." No one
ever summed up better those values and goals we share than your
president, Dick Lesher, 7 years ago. And no organization works
harder to advance human progress and freedom than the
U.S. Chamber under Dick's leadership, together with your State
and local chambers,-- and we thank you for all you're doing. Our
Administration deeply appreciates your decisive contributions,
helping us get this country back on track.

Someone else deserves special recognition today. For
31 years he has been with you -- a rock of stability and
integrity for the Chamber. He has lived the meaning of Abe
Lincoln's words: "Important principles may and must be
inflexible."

Bill Van Meter, I know you'll be retiring soon as Senior
Vice President, and I know you're up there somewhere. Would you
please stand up, and Dick Lesher too, so we can salute you both?

Now some may wonder, what does an organization do for an
encore, after it increases its membership 5-fold in 7 years,
creates an army of grassroots support, sets up its own magazine,
newspaper, and radio and television shows? Well, if I could make
a suggestion, our Administration still has a small problems as about 400 B/n
Capitol Hill we would love to have your help on. I think you
will help us, just like you did before. Accepting important
challenges is the Chamber's stock-in-trade, and a new one begins
today: How about the first business satellite television network

249

Page 3

system in the world -- a system that can reach every community in
this country to promote and strengthen our enterprise system?

My staff said this would be the first speech carried over
Biznet. Forgive me, I just had to ask them: Do you really think
the Chamber ~~wants me to do~~ *is ready for* another inaugural address already?

Well, what you are doing here, the tremendous growth you
have recently enjoyed, all underscores a truth too often ignored
in Washington: The most powerful force for progress in this
world does not come from Government elites, public programs, or
even precious resources like oil or gold. True wealth comes from
the heart; from the treasure of ideas and spirit; from the
investments of millions of brave people with hope for the future,
trust in their fellow men, and faith in God.

The American dream of human progress through freedom and
equality of opportunity in competitive enterprise is still the
most revolutionary idea in the world today. It is also the most
successful.

Entrepreneurs are heroes of modern times, but rarely receive
the credit they deserve. Treasury Secretary Don Regan recently
reminded the student body of Bucknell University: it was under
capitalism that mankind brought "light where before there was
darkness, heat where once there was only cold, medicines where
there was sickness and disease, food where there was scarcity,
and wealth where humanity was living in squalor." *And much of which
was happening about came into being in the life time of many of us here in this room*
INSERT →) The societies which achieve the most spectacular progress in
the shortest period of time are not the most tightly controlled,
the biggest in size, or the wealthiest in material resources.
*I have already lived about 20 yrs. longer than my life expectancy
at the time I was born. That's a source of annoyance to a great
many people.*

250

Page 4

They are revolut[...]

~~What unites them all is their willingness to~~ reward initiative ¶
to believe in the magic of the marketplace.

Trust the people -- that's the secret weapon. Only when
people are free to worship, create and build, only when they can
decide their destiny and benefit from their own risks -- only
then do societies become dynamic, prosperous, progressive and
free.

America has always done well when we had this courage to
believe in ourselves, our values and our capacity to perform
great deeds. We got into trouble when we listened to those who
insisted making Government bigger would make America better. Big
Government, they told us, was the wave of the future, and anyone
who stood in their way was a reactionary.

Not long ago, Senator Ted Kennedy paid tribute to former
Governor and Ambassador Averill Harriman, celebrating ~~a~~ birthday
I believe his 90th
~~last week~~. ~~Teddy Kennedy~~ *The Sen.* said Ambassador Harriman's age was *close to*
only half as old as Ronald Reagan's ideas. You know something --
he's absolutely right. The United States Constitution is almost
200 years old, and ~~that's where I get my ideas~~. *his ideas [...] get them...*

~~I happen to believe~~ Thomas Jefferson was no reactionary, ~~but~~
he was a true progressive when he warned: "the only safe depository of
the ultimate powers of society are with the people themselves."
The Tenth Amendment tells us: "The Federal Government will do
only those things called for in the Constitution and all others
with
shall remain with the States or the people." ← (?)

~~Would you not agree that~~ We have strayed much too far from
that noble beginning . . . that the whole purpose of our

251

Page 5

revolution -- personal freedom, equality of opportunity and
keeping Government close to the people -- is threatened by a
Federal spending machine that takes too much money from the
people, too much authority from ~~addresses~~ STATE & LOC. GOVTS., and ~~yes~~, too much
liberty with our Constitution?

We must preserve those first principles that made America
strong and will keep her free. ~~It's not a question of~~ That does not mean turning
back the clock, of retreating from Government's responsibility to
help those who cannot help themselves. ~~We will never abandon our~~ We are meeting our commitments
to the needy even if that hasn't been the subject of a network
~~commentary~~ documentary.
~~The policy by spotlighting individual cases of distress in a
Nation of 230 million, can leave the impression of a pattern of
neglect. This is untrue. I deeply regret any unnecessary
suffering but why no mention that~~ We now devote one of the
largest shares of the Federal budget in our history to assisting
low-income Americans? ~~Wouldn't that be fair? Why no mention~~
~~that~~ The growth policies of low spending and taxes of the
mid-60's were much better friends to the poor than the big
Government madness that followed and ~~that~~ WHICH created so much misery?
~~Speaking of misery that created the age of inflation with all the suffering
it brings to the poor & the elderly...~~
~~Or for the 1st time in 17 yrs. the...~~ 3.2
~~prices — 3.6% in Feb. 3.3% in March. For half a yr. it has averaged around 3.2%~~
inflation had ~~kept~~ running at the double digit rate it was ~~having
in 1980 & Jan. of 81~~
~~...~~, a family of four on a fixed income of $15,000
BE OVER
would $1,000 poorer in purchasing power than they are today.
~~I believe that is a newsworthy story.~~

Page 6

We are the most generous people on earth. I don't think any of us lack compassion for the needy. But isn't it time we also in compassion for those running hard who work and pay their tax

~~You have compassion for them. But though~~ *and their lives while they struggle to make ends meet?* ~~little compassion left over for the group Washington so often forgets -- the wage-earners and taxpayers of America?~~ They are

the heart and soul of the free enterprise system; ~~they pay America's bills; they have been burned by higher inflation and taxes year after year~~, and they need help ~~to~~.

Winston Churchill said that some see private enterprise as a predatory target to be shot, others as a cow to be milked, but few see it as the sturdy horse pulling the wagon. Well, this Administration believes the savers, investors and entrepreneurs of America have been milked and shot at long enough.

With your help, we're ending a long night of Government blundering and making an historic new beginning. *YES* ~~Certainly~~ we are in a painful recession. The unemployment are living a tragedy. ~~And~~ I want nothing more than to see them working again. *And* ~~But~~ I am convinced the course we have embarked on offers the best hope. I *certainly want* ~~can't~~ accept the idea that a program which ~~is just beginning~~, ~~which, in fact,~~ began *after* the recession was already underway, *somehow* is ~~responsible~~ for that recession. I hope we can reach a fair and bipartisan budget compromise. I will go the extra mile to reach an understanding with Members of the Congress, on both sides of the aisle, as long as a ~~critical~~ commitment to three essential priorities is maintained: continued rebuilding of our national defense; preservation of our tax incentives; and, a long-term effort to reduce the Federal Government's share of GNP, *which means getting this* ~~and getting this~~ budget under control once and for all.

253

Page 7

If there are

~~But to~~ those who shun any and all compromise, I must speak
plainly: We are not go~~ing~~ back to the glory days of big, *never mind the*
cut, Government, ~~and we will yield no quarter to big spenders~~. The
best view of ~~big~~ *that kind of* Government is in a rear view mirror as we leave
it behind.
We can no longer listen to those who say
If it's commerce, ~~they~~ regulate it. If it's income, ~~they~~
tax it. If it's a budget, ~~they~~ bust it. Given their way, they'd
make everything that isn't prohibited -- compulsory. *Will a bitter*
rule is — if it isn't easily don't give it.
~~Then when everything falls apart, they say it's because we~~
~~let them down. Until~~ We were not put on this Earth just to make
Government bigger. Our task is to restrain spending, create
incentives, provide hope, opportunities ↑ help our economy grow
again. Our loyalty will always be *to* ~~with~~ little taxpayers and
never ~~with~~ big taxspenders.

Our Administration promised a program of tax incentives so
industry could retool and families could save again for their
future. We have kept that promise *with the* ~~I introduce~~ first decent tax
reduction in nearly 20 years. ~~But the ink was barely dry when~~
Those
~~the~~ champions of big Government ~~expressed~~ *who have* 101 reasons why the
people's tax cut ~~has to~~ *must* go *exemplifying* ~~in~~ the words of Job in
the Good Book, they "multiplieth words without knowledge."
(To those who say)
~~Our tax cut is so massive, improper, it~~ will significantly
increase projected deficits ~~I say your wrong~~ *let me point out* Our tax cut *first*
has to
~~will barely~~ offset tax *increases* already built into the system,
including the Social Security tax increases passed in 1977 *— the largest*
single tax increase in our history.
Americans now shoulder the highest tax burden in peacetime
history *and there are a couple of more increases in that Soc. Security payroll*
tax yet to be be applied.

254

Page 8

~~You know I keep asking one question our critics won't~~
~~answer~~: If higher taxes are the key to reducing deficits, why
did a $300 billion tax increase between 1976 and 1981 leave us
with $318 billion in deficits?

I think you know why.
~~The Chamber of Commerce recently~~: We did not pile up a
                                                          have
trillion dollar debt because we're not taxed enough. We've ~~got~~
that debt because Government spends too much.
And what specifics can be given to support the repeated charge
~~that Some claim~~ our tax cut favors the wealthy. Seventy-four
percent of the tax savings goes to the lower and middle class who
presently pay 72 percent of the tax. May I just say, in the
quest for economic literacy: high tax rates don't soak the rich;
they only create more tax shelters, or an outright capital drain.
                                          s
~~By~~ Reducing high tax rates ~~we~~ provide incentives to get more
                                          ^
people paying taxes again. Just as important, we preserve one of
the few systems left on Earth where people at the bottom of the *ladder*
can still get rich.
~~People can reach for the stars, and I still believe~~ That's what
America should be all about. From now on, more of what people
earn belongs to them. ~~The age of redistribution and erosion of~~
~~freedom must end. We will reclaim our freedom; we will create~~
~~wealth again; we will not retreat from our historic reforms and~~
~~increase the tax burden of the American people.~~

Now, it's true that our program, just 6 months old, has not
solved all the economic problems we inherited. As Don Kendall
pointed out, our Administration did not have the luxury of
                                          such as we had
starting out with 6 percent interest rates, ~~as~~ back in 1977.
We were left with interest rates of 21½ percent -- the highest in
          and inflation was only half what it was in Jan. of 1981
more than a century. ~~And~~ It's a bit ironic to hear ~~the same~~

Page 9

~~those~~
~~people~~ who insisted the tax program be administered in drops
rather than spoonfuls, now saying the medicine didn't work. The
medicine will work when the patient finally begins to get it.
The first real dose begins with the 10 percent tax cut in July,
~~the~~ *of the* additional 10 percent cut in July of 1983. ~~We're going~~
~~to make sure that prescription is followed to the~~ letter.

I'm reminded of a time I testified before a Senate Committee
while I was still Governor of California. I was asked by one of
the committees why the President of my party had not corrected
everything that had gone wrong. I answered him with -- forgive
me -- an anecdote.

I told him about a ranch that Nancy and I had acquired. It
had a barn with six stalls where they had kept cattle, and we
wanted to keep horses. So I was in there day after day with a
pick axe and shovel, lowering the level of those stalls, which
had been raised by an accumulation over the years. I told the
Senator you could not undo in a few months what had been piling
up for years.

Now some in the media have ~~~~ the business community *(been telling us here in the Treasury)*
~~questions~~ ~~~~ the wisdom of our program. ~~~~ *I'm sure you can understand the*
hard that is on our morale. ~~~~ *Since the* ~~~~ Chamber
represents a great cross-section of the business community; ~~~~ I
wondered if I might ask you a few questions:

Number one Federal spending tripled in the last decade alone, and shot
up by 17 percent in 1980. Would you agree that by trying to
head down ~~~~ runaway spending, by trying to control those so-called

256

Page 10

budget items we've been told are
uncontrollable~~s~~, that we <u>are</u> doing the right thing and ~~that~~
~~we~~ should stick with it?

-- Taxes on the people doubled between 1976-1981, and would
have increased another $300 billion between 1981-1984
without our program. ~~Would you agree that~~ βy trying to
help families keep their heads above water, ~~by~~ refusing to
tax them like millionaires, ~~that we~~ <u>are</u> doing the right
thing, and ~~that we~~ should *we* stick with it?

-- Our program began *(as I said)* after the recession was underway. ~~But~~
~~when you realize what we've already accomplished~~ *Now with* -- growth
in spending cut nearly in half, regulation growth cut by a
third, inflation down *by almost 2/3* ~~dramatically~~, the prime rate down
5 percentage points, still too high but headed lower, and
strong new incentives to save ~~which are~~ just beginning --
~~would you agree that we~~ <u>are</u> *we* on the right road to a lasting
recovery and ~~that we~~ should *we* stick with it?

Well then, I have one more question: Will you mobilize your
240,000 members and tell the Congress what you just told me?

Every time personal tax rates go higher it becomes more
difficult for firms to compete in world markets. It now costs
$1.70 just to compensate a worker for *each* ~~every~~ $1.00 increase in the
cost of living. Instead of workers and management trying to
solve this problem by opposing each other, ~~I have a suggestion:~~
why not join forces, and *help us get* ~~tell this~~ Government ~~to get~~ off your
backs, so you can get on with the task of saving American jobs,
rebuilding our economy, and raising the standard of living of all
our people?

257

Page 11

With your personal initiative, ingenuity, industry and
responsibility we can make America work again -- you know we can.
But as we rebuild this blessed land, we'll need ~~something else~~
~~two~~ -- that extra dimension of faith, friendship, and brotherhood
that makes us good neighbors, ~~makes us~~ good people and makes
America a great country.

I believe standing up for America also means standing up for
the God who has so blessed this land. We have strayed so far; it
may be later than we think. There is a hunger in our land to see
traditional values reflected in public policy again. To those
who cite the First Amendment as reason for excluding God from
more and more of our institutions and everyday life, may I just
~~say~~ *point out*: The First Amendment of the Constitution was not written to
protect the people of this country from religious values -- it
was written to protect religious values from government tyranny.

One of America's greatest strengths is our tradition of
neighbor caring for neighbor in times of trouble. We have
launched a nationwide campaign to encourage citizens to join with
us, determine where need exists, then organize community
volunteer groups to meet those needs. A great challenge, and all
the more reason to have as Chairman of our Task Force on Private
Sector Initiatives, an individual we both know is an outstanding
leader -- Bill Verity, your own chairman a year ago.

Bill and I aren't asking you to take over the social welfare
system. We're just asking that you give generously of your time,
your know-how, and your imagination to help Americans help
themselves. Many of you already do. When we say Chamber of

258

Page 12

Commerce, what comes to mind: community leadership in economic development, job-creation, education, medical care and special assistance to the elderly, the disabled and the blind. ~~Don't~~ ~~tell us~~ American business doesn't care and is ~~not~~ involved. ~~Please,~~ Just keep doing what you do best, and ask more of those around you to pitch in and help.

A different kind of volunteer initiative is being taken by a *group of banks in Ohio & by the* the First National Bank of Plainfield, Indiana. ~~It~~ *They* recently lowered the interest rates on new car loans *(which were between 16 & 18%)* ~~to~~ to *between them some 15* 12 3/4 percent and committed ~~a~~ million to the program. In the *first few weeks the sale of new cars increased to several times what* ~~it~~ ~~had been its monthly average. The bankers involved said;~~ ~~had the previous month.~~ The ~~bank said the program might cost it~~ ~~some money, but that~~ "the financial sector has to pitch in and help" so we can get the economy moving again." ~~Wouldn't it be~~ ~~nice to read and hear a little more about this kind of community~~ ~~leadership by the business men and women of America?~~

Your 70th Annual Meeting is living proof that democracy and freedom are alive and well in America. But as you know, America is more the exception than the rule around the globe. Now some in this country say, "Freedom is fine for us, but we can't worry about it for everyone else." ~~Let ... necks out~~ *→ will* ~~anymore." ... have they forgotten that~~ freedom was not won here without the help of others? ~~Have they forgotten~~ *Whereever freedom is lost it is diminished everywhere and* ~~that people who turn their backs on freedom often ... what they~~ ~~cherish most for themselves. Have they forgotten that~~ freedom is never more than one generation from extinction?

17 15·

Having said this let me point out we are striving just as hard in the defense program to find savings and eliminate unnecessary spending as we are in every other dept. We believe such savings can be made without retreating from our effort to redress the imbalance that exists today.

I am also willing to look at additional revenue sources so long as they don't cancel out or erode the tax incentive measures for individuals & business that were adopted last year. And if there are alternative budget reductions to those we proposed in the '83 budget I'd like to hear them. The all important thing is for all of us here in Wash. to come to an agreement on how we are going to proceed toward a balanced budget. And then to stand together with no partisan difference dividing us and say; "here is the bipartisan solution we offer to our ec. problem.

Once this is done perhaps we can proceed to amend the Constitution so as to mandate a balanced budgets and then begin the reduction of the Nat. debt. Burning that mortgage will be the biggest fire since the burning of Rome.

Page 13

Francis Bacon wrote: ". . . in this theater of man's life
it is reserved only for God and angels to be lookers on."
America can not afford to drift through the 1980's as a
spectator. ~~Liberty belongs to the brave. We will stand up for~~
~~our ideals, and we will work for peace.~~ (I ~~trust you are as proud~~
~~as I am of the effort our country has made, led by Secretary~~
~~Haig, to prevent war between Great Britain and Argentina.)~~

One very important way the United States can contribute to
world peace is by helping stimulate international trade. The
assistance of the U.S. Chamber and your International Division in
developing new markets, more exports, and encouraging lower trade
barriers will continue to be invaluable. ~~to us.~~

It would be wonderful if we could secure peace through trade
alone. You and I know we cannot. We must restore the strength
of our armed forces which has been neglected for too long. ~~We~~
~~face a dangerous adversary which blatantly violates international~~
~~treaties and consistently seeks to expand its sphere of~~
~~influence.~~ The Soviet Union has deployed a military arsenal
unequalled in all history. ~~capable of confronting our allies in~~
~~Europe and Asia, and threatening the free world's source of oil.~~

~~I share the concerns about military waste and inefficiency.~~
~~We now have a plan to qualify that, and let me assure you -- no~~
~~area will be exempt.~~ The American people will no longer
tolerate a mere facade of security. They expect ~~their~~ planes to
fly, ~~their~~ ships to sail and ~~their~~ helicopters to stay aloft.
There will be no retreat in the commitment of this Administration
to make sure that they do. ~~We cannot bend in our efforts to~~
But again let me say this we must do as a
part of our effort to preserve the peace.

Page 14

~~repair our military and to regain a balance with the Soviet Union after only one year.~~

~~Let us ask those who say we are spending too much~~: How much
would ~~you~~ *we* have spent to avoid World War II? ~~Measured~~ *Can we* put a
price on the lives lost on Guadacanal, on Tarawa, Omaha Beach,
Anzio or Bastogne. Every penny we spend ~~is~~ *con defence* for one sacred
purpose: to prevent ~~our~~ *young* Americans ~~~~ *from having to shed up their blood in*
a war that could have been prevented.
~~foreign soil.~~ *While we rebuild our deteriorated national defense*
~~as you know~~, we are also working for essential reduction ~~of~~ *of*
the weapons of mass destruction. A freeze in the arsenals of
these weapons is not good enough. We ~~want to go one better~~ *must have* --
mutual and verifiable reductions *and this we shall strive for.*

Courage to stand up for American ideals, to work for peace,
to defend our freedom, and courage to follow through on the
economic recovery program begun last year -- courage to seize the
opportunities in this time of challenges. The famous French
diplomat Talleyrand once said, "Women sometimes forgive a man who
forces the opportunity, but never a man who misses one."

Let me take one more opportunity to say that we need a
bipartisan agreement on the budget. Should it turn out, however,
that the courage to restrain spending and hold down taxes is not
there, the American people do have alternatives. You can tell
the Congress, especially the Speaker, that there can be an
agreement if he is willing to be more flexible; and, you can
express your opinions at the ballot box next November; and you
can join the grassroots movement to pass a Constitutional

Page 15

Amendment that would mandate the Federal Government bring
spending down in line with revenues.

This Nation has no mission of mediocrity. We were never
meant to be second-best. The spirit that built our country was
bold, not timid. It was a spirit of pride, confidence and
courage that we could do anything. Well, we still can. ~~Today,
I'm appealing to you: ignore the cynics, ignore the prophets~~ of
~~failure who are paralyzed with fear. Set your sights on number~~
~~one, and together -- let's go for it.~~

I do not believe for one minute that America's best days are
behind her. I do not believe any of you doubt, that with the
right tools and incentives to do the job, we can and will be
every bit as skilled, and dedicated and productive as our German
and Japanese counterparts. America's greatest moments have
always come when we dared to be great -- when we believed in
ourselves and we reached out to each other to do the impossible.

We have come so far, we have done so much, and all in so
short a time. Let's not turn back now.

In his poem "Columbus," James Russell Lowell wrote of that
momentuous voyage across the Atlantic. The crew had been told
again and again they would soon see land on the horizon. They
saw only water. They were tired, ~~they were~~ hungry, ~~they were~~
lonely, ~~they were~~ desperate & ready to mutiny, ~~and risk going all~~
~~the way back~~.

But as Lowell wrote: ". . .Endurance is the crowning
quality, and patience all the passion of great hearts. . . ~~One~~
~~faith against a whole earth's unbelief . . . . One poor day~~!

Page 16

R~~emember whose and not how short it is! It is God's day, it is~~
~~Columbue~~'s. . . One day, with life and heart, is more than time
enough to find a world."

With your courage, your faith, your help, we can endure and
we can prevail. We can find that world and bequeath peace and
prosperity to our children and their children. ~~And it is because~~
~~I believe so much in you, that~~ I know we will.

Thank you for this wonderful morning. And God Bless you,
~~we're together, all the way in victo~~ry.

Appendix Two:
Where To Find Jokes and Quotes

The biggest problem with collections of jokes and quotes is that there are too many of them. Each has its unique merits as well as shortcomings. So, rather than provide an exhaustive list, I would like to share with you the handful of resources which I find most useful. These books contain both serious and humorous material.

The Forbes Scrapbook of Thoughts on the Business of Life. New York: Forbes, Inc., 1976.

America the Quotable. Edelhart, Mike and James Tinen, eds. New York: Facts on File Publications, 1983.

The Executive's Quotation Book. Charleton, James, ed. New York: St. Martin's Press, 1983.

Peter's Quotations. Peter, Laurence J. New York: Bantam Books, 1977.

The Toastmaster's Treasure Chest. Prochnow, Herbert V. and Herbert V. Prochnow, Jr. New York: Harper & Row, 1979.

10,000 Jokes, Toasts and Stories. Copeland, Lewis and Faye, eds. Garden City, New York: Doubleday & Co., Inc., 1965.

Business and Economic Quotations. Jackman, Michael, ed. New York: Macmillan Publishing Company, 1984.

The Little, Brown Book of Anecdotes. Fadiman, Clifton, ed. Boston: Little, Brown & Company, 1985.

Morrow's International Dictionary of Contemporary Quotations. Green, Jonathan, ed. New York: William Morrow & Company, 1982.

Appendix Three:
Some Jokes and Anecdotes
Worth Stealing

Go to any decent bookstore and you will find joke books by the dozens. That's the easy part. The hard part is finding and properly utilizing jokes that work.

The selection here is obviously not exhaustive or original. But an entertaining speech usually requires only one or two gems, and you might find them here. I have heard nearly all of these jokes draw laughs from audiences.

These stories are listed in no particular order, and many need to be "fine-tuned" to fit into your text and correspond with your themes. However, I have roughly divided them into the following categories:

Icebreakers - designed for the beginning of a speech, usually making fun of speakers who talk too long;

Thematic anecdotes – focused on contemporary topics as well as humor at the expense of society's favorite foibles, such as government, economists, and fiscal irresponsibility;

Parting Shots – poke fun at other systems of government or at pessimists about the future as a way of setting up a stirring, patriotic, optimistic, rhetorical conclusion.

Icebreakers

A new preacher was disappointed to find that only one member of the congregation showed up to hear his sermon. So he asked the parishioner, who was a farmer, "Should I go ahead with my sermon?"

The farmer said, "Well, I don't know about that sort of thing, but I do know this. If I loaded up a truck with hay, took it out to the prairie, and only one cow showed up, I'd feed her."

So the preacher took that advice and proceeded to deliver a sermon that lasted an hour and a half. When he was done, he asked the farmer, "What did you think?"

"Well, I don't know about that sort of thing, but I do know this," came the reply. "If I loaded up a truckload of hay, took it out to the prairie, and only one cow showed up, I sure wouldn't give her the whole load."

I'm reminded of the story about the Roman emperor centuries ago who gathered thousands of his subjects in the coliseum to witness some executions. When the first victim was thrown to the lions, the crowd roared its approval. But, as the lions approached, the prisoner whispered something in their ears, and they just turned around and walked away.

The emperor was furious. "Throw another one in there," he said. But the same thing happened. The second prisoner whispered something into the lions' ears and they just turned and walked away. Finally, after a few more tries, the emperor gave up. He went down to the dungeon and asked the prisoners, "What the heck are you telling those lions?" The first prisoner replied, "I just told them that there would be speeches after lunch!"

I'm starting to see the wisdom of the fellow who pointed out that there is something good to be said about making statues out of politicians — at least the statues keep their mouths shut!

I'm reminded of the senator who was warned by a reporter, "Sir, your constituents were confused by your speech today." The Senator replied, "Good. It took me eight hours to write it that way."

They tell the story about the long-winded senator who traveled all the way from Washington, D.C., to his home state to witness a public hanging that was attended by thousands of citizens. The condemned man was offered five minutes to say his last words. When he refused the privilege, the senator stood up and said, "Would you yield your five minutes to me?" The prisoner replied, "Sure, as long as they hang me first!"

268

I will be brief, but not quite as brief as the cub reporter who was assigned to write some obituaries. He submitted one to his editor that went like this: "Mr. Jones looked up the elevator shaft to see if it was on the way down. It was. Age forty-five."

They tell the story about the sheriff of a small town who became suspicious of the resident who made his living selling fish to local restaurants. It seems that this fellow was always able to catch more fish than anyone else. So, one day, he decided to go with the fisherman to see what his secret was. When they got out to the middle of the lake, the fisherman pulled out a stick of dynamite, lit the fuse, tossed it overboard, and with the explosion, up came the fish.

The sheriff was shocked and said, "Don't you realize you just committed a felony?" The fisherman reached down into his tackle box, took out another stick of dynamite, lit the fuse, and handed it to the sheriff, saying, "Did you come here to fish or to talk?"

I'm not going to speak very long this evening. I stopped doing that when I found out that George Washington gave an Inaugural Address that was less than 150 words, and he turned out to be a great leader. On the other hand, President William Henry Harrison gave a two-hour address in a snowstorm. He caught a cold and left office after a month!

I'd like to make just a few remarks this evening. I think the Wright brothers had the right idea when it came to speeches. At one of the many banquets in their honor, the host asked Wilbur to take the podium and say a few words. He got up very nervously and said, "There must be some mistake. Orville is the one who does the talking." So, then Orville got up and said, "Wilbur just made the speech."

I don't plan to speak for very long. They tell the story about the time Mark Twain arrived in a strange town to make a speech. When he stopped in at the barbershop, the barber, who didn't recognize him, said, "You picked a good time to visit. That fellow Mark Twain is going to make a speech tonight. But I have to warn you, every seat has already been sold. It's standing room only." And Mark Twain replied, "That's just my luck. Every time that fellow makes a speech, I have to stand!"

I don't plan to speak very long this evening. I'm reminded of the time that Albert Einstein was asked to explain his formula for success. In his most professorial tone, he said, "Suppose "a" stands for success. Then my formula is: $a = x + y + z$. The "x" stands for work, the "y" stands for play, and the "z" stands for keeping your mouth shut."

As Thomas Jefferson wisely pointed out, "A speech that is measured by the hour will die within the hour."

Seeing this big crowd reminded me of the time that Winston Churchill was asked if he didn't get impressed with himself because the hall was packed every time he made a speech. Churchill said, "No, every time it starts going to my head, I remind myself that, if instead of making a speech I was being hanged, the crowd would be twice as big!"

Thomas Jefferson once said, "It is the trade of lawyers to question everything, yield nothing, and talk by the hour." I'll try to avoid that third tendency today.

I'm reminded of Winston Churchill's warning that there are only two things more difficult than giving a speech after lunch: climbing a fence that's leaning toward you, or kissing a pretty girl who's leaning away from you.

Thematic Anecdotes

Why do defense contractors' costs run so high? According to the *Wall Street Journal*, Army Secretary James Ambrose returned a ten-inch stack of specifications for a helicopter engine and asked staffers to cut it in half. The pile returned, half as thick — because the bureaucrats had used both sides of the paper instead of one side.

Will Rogers once said, "Don't gamble. Take all your savings and buy some good stock and hold it till it goes up, then sell it. If it don't go up, don't buy it."

There was a town that decided they would have better traffic safety if they raised the height of their traffic signs from five to seven feet above the ground. But then, the federal government came in and said they had a plan to help them, and their plan was to lower the streets two feet.

Walter Heller, an economist for Presidents Kennedy and Johnson, said, "An economist is a person who, when he finds something that works in practice, wonders if it will work in theory."

Will Rogers once said, "An economist is a man who can tell you what can happen under any given set of circumstances, and his guess is liable to be as good as anyone else's."

Will Rogers said, "All our senators and congressmen are away from Washington now. This is the season of the year when they do the least damage to their country."

Babe Ruth was once challenged about his $80,000 salary, enormous for his day, when it was pointed out that he took in more for

271

hitting home runs than Hoover earned as President of the United States. The Babe replied, "Yeah, but I had a better year than Hoover did."

Senator Sam Ervin, after voting against a bill to allow the teaching of evolution in North Carolina public schools, explained that, "The monkeys in the jungle will be pleased to know that the North Carolina legislature has absolved them from any responsibility for humanity."

I'm reminded of the story about the farm couple from the Midwest who went to Italy. The guide was telling them about a volcano and the tremendous heat and fire that spewed forth when it erupted. The old boy just listened as long as he could and then, finally, said: "We got a volunteer fire department back home, put that thing out in fifteen minutes."

They tell the story about the automobile accident in which there was an injured man stretched out on the ground. A woman was hovering over him trying to give him some aid. A crowd started to gather, and then a man elbowed his way through and pushed the woman aside, saying, "Let me at him. I've had first aid training." The woman stepped back and watched for awhile. Finally, she tapped the man on the shoulder and said, "When you come to the part about calling the doctor, I'm right here."

If you think old soldiers fade away, just try getting into your old uniform.

That approach reminds me of the story Mark Twain once told about how he rescued Old Man Hankinson, who was trapped on the fourth floor of a burning house. He said, "Everyone was beside themselves because none of the ladders was long enough to reach that poor old man. So, I got a bright idea. I got a rope and I flung it up to Old Man Hankinson and yelled, 'Tie it around your waist.' He did so and then I pulled him down."

A wise person once said that the reason why most Capitol buildings have a rotunda is so that politicians have a place to run around in circles.

They tell the story about a man who found that his Social Security checks stopped coming. So, he went to the Social Security office to complain. The bureaucrat told him that the reason his checks had stopped was that the computer said he is dead. The man replied, "Well, you can see that I'm not dead, so give me my check." The bureaucrat said, "I'm sorry. If the computer says you're dead, then you're dead. But, just to show you that we're reasonable people, we'll give you your Social Security funeral allowance to tide you over."

Speaking about our economy reminds me of the conversation that was overheard outside a classroom at one of our great universities. The student asked his teacher, "Do you mean to tell me that the freest, fairest, and most productive economic system known to mankind is based on private ownership and the profit motive?" The teacher said, "That's right, it's called free enterprise." And then the student said, "But isn't there some solution to this?"

They tell the story about the law they once had on the books in Kansas which said, "If two trains reach an intersection at the same time, both shall come to a complete stop, and neither shall move again until the other is gone!"

They tell the story about two friends who were hiking in the woods. Suddenly, they crossed paths with a very hungry grizzly bear. Quickly, one of the friends puts on a pair of tennis shoes. The other said, "Don't be ridiculous. You can't outrun that bear." And he replied, "I know that, but I don't have to outrun the bear. I just have to outrun you!"

I'm reminded of the story about the young socialist who called on the wealthy banker, Baron Rothschild, to argue for a more equitable distribution of income. The Baron listened calmly, took pencil and paper in hand, and proceeded to divide his total wealth by the current world population. He then called his secretary and said, "Would you please give this young man sixteen cents. That is his share of my wealth."

They tell the story about one of those famous Lincoln-Douglas debates. Douglas thought he could score points by reminding the audience about Lincoln's previous employment selling whiskey and cigars. Well, they didn't call him Honest Abe for nothing. Lincoln admitted it was true. He used to be a bartender. But, he also told the audience that, "In those days, Mr. Douglas was one of my very best customers. The difference between us now is that I've left *my* side of the counter, but Mr. Douglas still sticks as tenaciously as ever to his."

Robert Frost once said, "The brain is a marvelous instrument. It starts working the moment you get up in the morning, and it doesn't stop until you get to the office!"

The late billionaire J. Paul Getty once said, "If you can count your money, then you don't have a billion dollars."

Most people might agree with the sentiments of Will Rogers when he told the story about a senator who accused his colleagues of being a bunch of wild jackasses. Will said, "If you think the senators were mad, just wait till the jackasses find out how they have been slandered!"

I'm reminded of Will Rogers' words of consolation. He said, "Just be thankful you aren't getting *all* the government you're paying for."

Will Rogers once said, "The income tax has made more liars out of the American people than golf has."

Sometimes I think government is like that old definition of a baby: an enormous appetite on one end and no sense of responsibility on the other.

They tell the story about three businessmen who were sitting around talking about the definition of fame. "Fame," the first man said, "is when you're invited to the White House for a personal chat with the President." The second man said, "Not so. Fame is when you're invited to the White House for a personal chat with the President, the red phone rings, and the President ignores it." But the third man disagreed with them both. "Fame is when you're invited to meet with the President. The red phone rings. The President picks it up and says it's for you!"

They tell the story about the attorney Mr. Jones, who, upon his death, met St. Peter at the Pearly Gates. St. Peter said, "It seems, Mr. Jones, that you've had a long and rewarding life. You've lived to be 106." "There must be some mistake," the lawyer exclaimed. I died at 56. You called me up too soon!" St. Peter replied, "I've been adding up all your time sheets, Mr. Jones, and you could not have been a day less than 106."

Some of you may have heard the story about the farmer who wrote to the Department of Agriculture, and it read, "Dear Sirs, something is wrong with my chickens. Every morning when I come out, I find two or three more lying on the ground cold and stiff, with their feet up in the air. Can you tell me what's wrong?" Eight weeks later, he received a reply from Washington: "Dear Sir, your chickens are dead."

_____

I'm reminded of the tourists who were peering down into the Grand Canyon. Their guide told them, "It took millions and millions of years for this great abyss to be carved out." And one tourist replied, "Really? I didn't know this was a government job!"

_____

Those million dollar lotteries have been in the news a lot lately. They remind me of the time a farmer won a million dollars, and he was asked what he planned to do with the money. He said, "I'm just going to keep on farming until it's all gone."

_____

They tell the story about the salesman who tried to sell a housewife a new freezer by saying, "Just think how much money you can save on your food bills." And the woman replied, "I know that. But, you see, we're paying for our compact car on the gas we save. We're paying for our washer and dryer on the laundry bills we save, and we're paying for the house on the rent we save. We just can't afford to save any more right now."

_____

This pressure reminds me of the life insurance agent who was very anxious to sell a policy to a new client. He said, "I don't want to pressure you into this, so why don't you sleep on it tonight — and *if* you wake up tomorrow, you can give me your answer then."

_____

They tell the story about the time that a surgeon, an architect, and a politician were engaged in a heated argument about whose profession was the oldest. The surgeon claimed that it was his because, according to the Bible, "Eve was made from Adam's rib — and that feat surely would have required surgery." But the architect argued that, before that, order was created out of chaos — and that was an architectural job. At which point the politician interrupted and said, "That's right, but who do you think created the chaos?"

_____

Parting Shots

In 1899, the head of the U.S. Patent office proposed that his office be closed, because everything that can be invented has already been invented. Then he got on his horse and rode home!

___

With the advent of sound tracks for motion pictures in the 1920s, Harry Warner of Warner Brothers was unimpressed. He said, "Who the hell wants to hear actors talk?"

___

Did you know that Fulton tried to sell his steamships to Napolean to be turned into warships? But Napoleon replied, "Are you telling me that you can make a ship go against the tide and the wind and the current by building a bonfire under the deck? I won't listen to such foolishness!"

___

In 1921, Tris Speaker of the Cleveland Indians baseball team said this: "Babe Ruth made a big mistake when he gave up pitching."

___

They tell the story about the two fellows in the Soviet Union who were walking down the street, and one of them says, "Have we really achieved full communism?" And the other said, "Oh, hell, no. Things are going to get a lot worse."

___

They tell the story about Woodrow Wilson who tried so mightily at the end of World War I to get all nations to adhere to his fourteen-point plan for peace. He died before this could become a reality. When he got to heaven, he was met by Moses, who told him, "Woodrow, you wouldn't believe what a mess they're making down there of your fourteen points." And the President replied, "Moses, that's nothing compared to what they're doing to your ten commandments."

___

Some years ago, King Carol of Romania selected fourteen of the brightest young people in his country for training in government service. He sent seven of them to England and seven to America to study the systems of the two countries. When asked what happened, the King said, "The seven who went to England became very wise and they all have important jobs in Bucharest. But the seven we sent to America were even wiser — they stayed in America."

They tell the story of the two shoppers who were in a fish market and they noticed two barrels filled with lobsters. One barrel said, "Lobsters, $10.00 a pound." The other said, "Lobsters, $20.00 a pound." As they watched, one of the lobsters in the $10.00 barrel struggled to climb to the top, teeter on the edge for a second, and then fall into the $20.00 barrel. One shopper turned to the other and said, "You know, this could only happen in America!"

I understand that the Soviet Union is planning a million dollar lottery of its own. The winners get a dollar a year for a million years!

They tell the story about the Russian and the American who were arguing about the respective virtues of their nations. The American said, "I can stand on any street corner in my country and freely criticize the President of the United States." And the Russian replied, "Big deal. I can stand on any street corner in *my* country and criticize the President of the United States, too!"

A few years ago, Fidel Castro was making a speech to a huge crowd in Havana. But a vendor walking through the crowd kept interrupting by shouting, "Peanuts, Popcorn!" Finally, Fidel got so mad that he said, "Bring me that man who keeps shouting peanuts and popcorn, and I'll kick him all the way to Miami." And the whole crowd started yelling, "Peanuts, Popcorn!"

Appendix Four:
Sample Speech Openings
and Conclusions

Governor Deukmejian speaking to the Los Angeles Rotary Club

(Opening)

Thank you very much, Bob, and good afternoon ladies and gentlemen. It is a genuine pleasure to be here with all of you today.

I would like to take this opportunity to commend Rotary Five for all that you are doing to make this community a better place to live and work. Through your generous scholarship and service programs for young people, and contributions to such worthy efforts as the Boy Scout Camp at Lake Arrowhead, the Crippled Children's Society, the Downtown Women's Center, and the YMCA, to name just a few, you've brightened the lives of so many fellow citizens. Your commitment to voluntary service is proof positive that Californians are people who care.

Right before I came up to speak, one of your members said to me, "Duke, we've been waiting a long time for a speaker who can dazzle us with charm, wit, and personality. I guess we can wait a little longer."

I promise not to speak for too long this afternoon. It's worth noting that the Lord's Prayer is only 56 words long. The Gettysburg Address is 226. The Ten Commandments are 297. But the U.S. Department of Agriculture's order on the price of cabbage is 15,629 words. I'll try to finish somewhere in between!

With common sense as our guide, in three years we have gone from a state whose government continually *gave* California the business, to a government that *brings* business to California . . . .

(Conclusion)

We are committed to a California that helps people in need, but we are striving to build a California where fewer people need help.

We've come a long way in three years. We have a long way to go. The freedom we cherish, the hope we hold for a prosperous future, and the helping hand we offer to our fellow citizens are ideals we all share. I urge you to help us build a society filled with safety, opportunity, and educational growth for every resident. God willing, we will make California and America strong and prouder than ever before.

Thank you very much.

Lawyer speaking to area bar association

(Opening)

Thank you very much, Joe (person who introduced you), and good afternoon ladies and gentlemen. It's great to be here and see so many good friends. I'd like to express my gratitude to the officers of the Midland Bar Association for giving me this opportunity.

I promise not to speak too long. Thomas Jefferson once said, "It is the trade of lawyers to question everything, yield nothing, and talk by the hour." I'll resist that last temptation today.

While I'm quoting great figures of the past, let me also share with you the immortal words of William Shakespeare. Over 300 years ago he wrote, "First thing we do is kill all the lawyers."

Well, according to recent opinion surveys, the public may not want to go *that* far, but they do hold our profession in very low esteem. I'd like to explore some of the reasons for that and suggest what we can do about it here in Midland.

(Conclusion)

Ladies and gentlemen, they tell the story about Justice Oliver Wendell Holmes, in which the distinguished jurist was riding on a train and couldn't find his ticket. The conductor told him not to worry, he could send it in when he found it. Holmes looked at the conductor with some irritation and said, "The problem is not where my ticket is. The problem is where am I going?"

Where our profession is going is a question that should concern each of us. America was arguably the first society to be governed according to the rule of law and not according to the capricious whims of warlords or the birthrights of monarchs. You and I have taken a solemn oath to uphold the law, to nurture it and protect it, and to perform our duties according to the highest ethical standards.

Ours is a great profession. We have nothing to be ashamed of. But at this critical juncture, with our credibility under attack, we have a duty to cross-examine ourselves with the same scrutiny that we cross-examine unfriendly witnesses on the stand.

Today I have discussed the questions we should be asking of ourselves and I have suggested some changes we should be making. Rather than lower our sights, we must raise our professional standards. It is within our power to restore the public's faith in lawyers. And when we do that we will have helped restore the public's faith in America's most cherished legacy to the cause of human liberty, the rule of law.

Thank you very much.

Entrepreneur speaking to local Chamber/Rotary

(Opening)

Thank you very much, Susan (name of person introducing you), and good afternoon ladies and gentlemen. This is a thrilling experience for me. Growing up in this community, I looked up to so many of you because you represented the kind of businessperson I wanted to be.

Now, I'm being honored by you as entrepreneur of the year. I really appreciate it, but the real honor belongs to the Hometown Chamber of Commerce and all of you. The Hometown business community stands for more than just turning a profit. You stand for opportunity and a good quality of life for our neighbors. You believe in education, as evidenced by your college scholarship program for students who might not otherwise get the chance to attend.

I know. I was one of them. And for that, I will be forever grateful.

As a small token of my gratitude, I'm going to do you a big favor and not speak for very long. I'll be brief, but not quite as brief as the cub reporter who was assigned by his editor to write some obituaries. He turned one in that said, "Mr. Jones looked up the elevator shaft to see if it was on its way down. It was. Age 45."

Well, it doesn't take a lot of words to tell you what I believe small business needs to make a go of it in today's economy . . . .

(Conclusion)

Ladies and gentlemen, the inventor and entrepreneur Thomas Edison devised many successful formulas, but my favorite is this one: "The three great essentials to achieve anything worthwhile," he said, "are first, hard work; second, stick-to-itiveness; and third, common sense."

Involvement in the political process is critical. As I've suggested today, if private enterprise doesn't join the fray and defend the system that gives us the freedom to grow and innovate, who is going to do it for us?

Yet, when all is said and done, we can't blame government for our problems and we must not look to government for the solutions. Whether we succeed or fail depends on our hard work, stick-to-itiveness, and common sense. It means being true to those simple verities of good business: innovation, quality, and integrity.

Every successful business, no matter how small, makes an important contribution to our community. We provide essential services, we provide jobs, and we provide living proof to our children that the American dream is alive and well in Hometown.

Thank you very much.

Community leader talking to charitable organization

(Opening)

Thank you very much, John (name of person introducing you), and good morning ladies and gentlemen. I appreciate this opportunity to share my views with the Hometown Benevolent Society.

I know that listening to a speech this early in the morning is not the easiest thing to do. It was Robert Frost who said, "The brain is a remarkable instrument. It starts working the moment you get up in the morning . . . and it doesn't quit until you get to the office."

You know, we have a lot to be proud of in this community. Our downtown shopping area has been revitalized. This new community center has attracted a variety of new cultural and athletic events to our town. Business leaders around the nation know that Hometown welcomes responsible growth and new jobs, and last year we attracted more new business expansions than any other comparable community in the country.

Yet growth must have a reason. Progress must have a purpose. I'd like to suggest to you today that all the prosperity in the world will be meaningless if we continue to leave part of our community behind and if we neglect to improve the daily quality of life for all our residents.

Today, I'd like to share with you what my company is doing to improve the lives of Hometown residents . . . .

(Conclusion)

Ladies and gentlemen, I feel like I've been preaching to the choir this morning. Through your dedicated efforts as members of the Hometown Benevolent Association, you have bettered the lives and brightened the hopes of thousands of our friends and neighbors.

Your spirit is unbeatable and it is spreading like a prairie fire through the heart of our community. Today, more residents are spending more of their time and money to help the disadvantaged than ever before. Voluntarism, that secret American weapon that helped the pioneers tame a wild continent, is alive and well in Hometown.

This is a community on the rise. Our future has never been brighter. In the years to come, we are going to cross exciting new frontiers of progress and prosperity. But this time, we're not going to leave anyone behind.

Thank you very much.

Index

EXCITING PRODUCTS – ESPECIALLY
SELECTED FOR READERS OF THIS BOOK . . .

As a reader of this book, you are already way ahead of most other communicators. To help you further increase your C.Q. (Communication quotient), we have put together an unbeatable combination of books, videos, and tapes to help you become a master communicator.

The following materials combine the best available information on personal communication, offering you a do-it-yourself graduate course in powerful communications. A "must" for anyone who wants to be a leader!

WO-1 **TV/PR**. Written by Emmy award-winning TV producers, Wicke Chambers and Spring Asher, this is the definitive book on how to get yourself, your company, or your cause on television. Includes vital information on how to prepare for your interview, look your best, and be invited back again and again .. $24.95 US

WO-2 **COMMUNICATE WHAT YOU THINK**. Written by Earl Nightingale, this six-cassette album will show you how to transmit your thoughts to others without sacrificing meaning or intent. The material is organized into 20 fact-filled and enjoyable audio sessions.. $65.00 US

WO-3 **PERSUASIVE SPEAKING VIDEO**. Produced by the publishers of *Esquire*, this VHS program will show you: How to size up an audience, eliminate stage fright and nervous speech habits, use eye contact and body language. Included are clips of master speakers, including JFK and Lee Iacocca. This invaluable cassette program will help you make memorable, action-inspiring presentations .... $29.95 US

WO-4 **COMMUNICATIONS POWER PACK – SAVE $20!!!**
Ordered separately, the above 3 items would cost $119.90. Order all 3 together — the complete Communications Power Pack — and save $20! .... $99.90 US

OTHER EXCITING EDUCATIONAL TOOLS FOR EXECUTIVES:

WO-5, WO-6 SEVEN STRATEGIES FOR WEALTH AND HAPPINESS – Jim Rohn

Jim Rohn, one of the best-known business philosophers and Executive International Director of Herbalife, shares the "fundamentals" of success, step by step. If you've ever suspected that your mosaic of *balanced* success is missing a piece, then Jim Rohn has the answer for you!

WO-5 Book .... $13.95 US
WO-6 Six-cassette Album .... $65.00 US

ORDER FORM

Dear People at Prima: I'd like to order the following items:

Quantity	#	Title	Unit Cost	TOTAL
_____	WO-1	TV/PR	$24.95*	$_____
_____	WO-2	Communicate What You Think	$65.00*	$_____
_____	WO-3	Persuasive Speaking Video	$29.95*	$_____
_____	WO-4	POWER PACK (all 3 above)	$99.90*	$_____
_____	WO-5	Seven Strategies (Book) ..	$13.95*	$_____
_____	WO-6	Seven Strategies (Cassettes)	$65.00*	$_____

Subtotal .... $_____

CA sales tax (if applicable) .... $_____

Shipping: Allow 4 weeks. (Foreign orders: we charge
exact air mail postage to your Visa/MC plus $3 handling) $_____

TOTAL TO BE REMITTED .... $_____

*A great gift idea!

HOW TO ORDER: By telephone: With Visa/MC, call (916) 624-5718.
Phone orders are taken Mon.-Fri., 9 a.m.-4 p.m. Pacific time.

By Mail: Just fill out the information below and send with your
remittance.

I am paying by (check one): ☐ Check   ☐ MO   ☐ Visa/MC.

My name is _____

I live at _____

City _____ State _____ Zip _____

Visa/MC # _____ Expiration _____

Signature _____

PRIMA PUBLISHING
POST OFFICE BOX 1260JR
ROCKLIN, CA 95677
(Satisfaction unconditionally guaranteed.)